AIR FRYER
COOKBOOK

2000 Days of Amazingly Quick, Delicious & Easy
Air Fryer Recipes for Beginners and Average Home Cooks

BY JACK CARTER

Disclaimer and Terms of Use:

Effort has been made to ensure that the information in this book is accurate and complete, however, the author and the publisher do not warrant the accuracy of the information, text and graphics contained within the book due to the rapidly changing nature of science, research, known and unknown facts and internet. The Author and the publisher do not hold any responsibility for errors, omissions or contrary interpretation of the subject matter herein. This book is presented solely for motivational and informational purposes only.

TABLE OF CONTENTS

INTRODUCTION

Greetings, Air Fryer Enthusiasts!

Welcome to a world of sizzling sensations, culinary creativity, and healthier cooking with the Air Fryer Cookbook. Whether you're a seasoned kitchen pro or a novice cook, this book is your ticket to unlocking the full potential of your air fryer. Get ready to embark on a culinary journey that will revolutionize the way you prepare and enjoy your favorite dishes.

The air fryer has taken the cooking world by storm, and for good reason. It's a kitchen appliance that combines the magic of frying with the science of hot air circulation. The result? Crispy, golden perfection without the excess oil and guilt that often accompanies deep frying. From crispy fries to succulent chicken wings and even delectable desserts, the possibilities are endless.

In this cookbook, we'll delve deep into the world of air frying, exploring its origins, how it works, and the numerous benefits it brings to your kitchen. You'll also find a treasure trove of recipes, cooking tips, and maintenance advice that will make you an air fryer maestro in no time.

So, if you're ready to elevate your cooking game, reduce your oil intake, and tantalize your taste buds, join us on this delicious journey through the world of air frying. Let's get started!

WHAT TO EXPECT FROM THIS AIR FRYER BOOK

Discovering the contents and expectations of this Air Fryer Cookbook is your first step towards becoming an air frying aficionado. We've curated this culinary adventure to provide you with a comprehensive guide to all things air frying. Here's a sneak peek of what you can expect:

- **Mouthwatering Recipes:** Our cookbook is brimming with a diverse range of recipes, from classic comfort foods to innovative creations. Whether you're craving crispy appetizers, juicy main courses, or delightful desserts, we've got you covered.

- **In-Depth Knowledge:** Dive into the world of air fryers with detailed explanations of how they work, their benefits, and practical cooking tips. You'll gain a deeper understanding of this remarkable kitchen appliance.

- **Healthy Cooking:** Learn how to prepare your favorite dishes with significantly less oil, reducing calories without sacrificing flavor. Discover the art of guilt-free indulgence.

- **Time-Saving Techniques:** Harness the power of the air fryer's rapid cooking capabilities to whip up meals in a fraction of the time it would take with conventional cooking methods.

- **Maintenance and Care:** Extend the life of your air fryer by following our maintenance tips and cleaning routines. A well-maintained appliance ensures consistent, high-quality results.

- **Cooking Confidence:** Whether you're a beginner or an experienced cook, our cookbook provides step-by-step instructions and tips that will boost your culinary confidence and inspire your inner chef.

- **Creative Inspiration:** Get creative in the kitchen with recipes that will spark your imagination. Experiment with flavors, ingredients, and techniques to craft unique dishes your family and friends will love.

As you explore the chapters of this cookbook, you'll unlock the secrets to successful air frying and discover a world of delicious possibilities. So, roll up your sleeves, put on your apron, and let's embark on this exciting culinary adventure together.

WHAT IS AN AIR FRYER?

Before we dive into the tantalizing recipes and culinary delights that the air fryer can create, let's start with the basics: What exactly is an air fryer?

An air fryer is a revolutionary kitchen appliance that has taken the culinary world by storm. It's designed to mimic the results of deep frying without the need for excessive oil. Instead of submerging your food in a vat of hot oil, the air fryer uses hot air circulation to achieve that coveted crispy texture on the outside while keeping the inside tender and moist.

The core components of an air fryer include a heating element, a powerful fan, and a cooking basket. When you set the desired temperature and cooking time, the heating element generates intense heat, while the fan circulates this hot air rapidly around the food. This continuous circulation ensures even cooking and browning, giving you that perfect crunch.

One of the standout features of an air fryer is its versatility. It can tackle a wide range of dishes, from traditionally fried foods like French fries and chicken wings to healthier options like roasted vegetables and baked goods. In essence, an air fryer is a compact, all-in-one kitchen workhorse that can perform tasks typically reserved for ovens, deep fryers, and even grills.

While the concept of air frying may seem like a recent innovation, the roots of this cooking method trace back to the 1960s. However, it wasn't until more recent years that air fryers became a household staple, thanks to their user-friendly designs and the growing desire for healthier cooking alternatives.

So, why has the air fryer gained such popularity? Let's explore some of the key advantages it offers in the next chapter.

HOW DOES THE
AIR FRYER WORK?

The inner workings of an air fryer are a fascinating blend of technology and culinary innovation. Understanding how it works is the key to mastering this versatile kitchen appliance.

At its core, an air fryer relies on the principles of convection cooking. Convection ovens have been around for a while, but the air fryer takes this concept to a whole new level of efficiency and convenience.

Here's a step-by-step breakdown of how an air fryer works its magic:

1. Heating Element: When you set the desired cooking temperature on your air fryer, the heating element at the top of the appliance kicks into action. This element generates intense heat that serves as the energy source for cooking your food.

2. Fan Power: A powerful fan located above the heating element comes into play. This fan is responsible for rapidly circulating the hot air around the cooking chamber. The fan's high-speed operation ensures even distribution of heat, which is crucial for achieving that perfect crispiness.

3. Cooking Basket: Placed inside the cooking chamber, the food basket is where the magic happens. It's typically perforated to allow the hot air to reach every nook and cranny of your food. As the hot air circulates, it cooks your food from all sides simultaneously.

4. Food Preparation: Before placing your food in the air fryer, it's important to prepare it properly. This often involves lightly coating the food with a small amount of oil or using a cooking spray. This oil helps facilitate the browning process, creating that appealing crispy texture.

5. Crispy Perfection: As the hot air envelops your food, it rapidly removes moisture from the surface, creating a crispy exterior. Meanwhile, the heat penetrates the food, ensuring it cooks evenly from the inside out. This dual-action process results in dishes that are crispy on the outside and tender on the inside.

6. Cooking Control: Most air fryers come equipped with adjustable temperature and timer settings, allowing you to fine-tune your cooking to perfection. The timer ensures your food is cooked for just the right amount of time, while the temperature setting allows you to control the level of heat.

7. Ready to Serve: Once your food reaches golden perfection, the air fryer alerts you, and your meal is ready to be savored. No more messy oil baths, excessive splattering, or the need to babysit your food as it cooks.

Now that you have a grasp of how an air fryer operates, it's time to explore the myriad benefits it brings to your kitchen and your culinary adventures.

BENEFITS OF USING
AN AIR FRYER

The air fryer is more than just a trendy kitchen gadget; it's a game-changer for home cooks. Let's delve into the incredible benefits that come with using this remarkable appliance:

1. Healthier Cooking: Perhaps the most celebrated advantage of air frying is its ability to produce crispy, delicious food with significantly less oil. Traditional deep frying submerges food in large quantities of oil, leading to a calorie-laden meal. In contrast, air frying uses only a fraction of the oil while still delivering that satisfying crunch.

2. Reduced Fat Content: By cutting down on oil, air frying reduces the fat content of your meals. This is a boon for those watching their calorie intake or trying to make heart-healthy choices.

3. Crispy Texture: Air frying achieves that coveted crispy texture on the outside of your food without sacrificing moisture on the inside. You'll enjoy the crunch without the grease.

4. Versatility: Air fryers are incredibly versatile appliances. They can handle a wide range of foods, from classic fried favorites like chicken wings and onion rings to more health-conscious options like vegetable chips and grilled chicken breasts.

5. Speedy Cooking: Air fryers heat up quickly and cook food faster than conventional ovens. This means you can enjoy your favorite dishes in less time, making them perfect for busy weeknights.

6. Energy Efficiency: Air fryers are energy-efficient appliances that consume less power than traditional ovens. You'll save on electricity bills while reducing your carbon footprint.

7. Minimal Odor and Mess: Say goodbye to the lingering smell of deep-fried foods in your kitchen. Air frying produces minimal odors and leaves behind little mess, making cleanup a breeze.

8. Cooking Precision: Most air fryers come equipped with precise temperature and timer settings, allowing you to cook your food to perfection every time. No more guesswork or overcooked meals.

9. Healthier Meal Options: With an air fryer, you can enjoy your favorite comfort foods with a healthy twist. Try air-fried sweet potato fries, crispy kale chips, or guilt-free doughnuts.

10. Family-Friendly: Air fryers are a hit with the whole family. Kids love the crispy treats, and parents appreciate the healthier cooking method.

11. Recipe Adaptability: You can adapt many of your favorite recipes to the air fryer with ease. Experiment with different seasonings and ingredients to create unique dishes.

12. Reduced Kitchen Heat: During hot summer months, air frying is a welcome alternative to using a conventional oven, as it generates less heat in your kitchen.

13. Great for Small Spaces: Air fryers are compact and perfect for small kitchens or apartments where space is limited.

Now that you're well-versed in the benefits of air frying, you're ready to take your culinary skills to the next level. In the following chapters, we'll explore essential cooking tips, maintenance advice, and a wide array of scrumptious recipes that will leave your taste buds tingling with delight.

AIR FRYER COOKING TIPS

Becoming a master of air frying requires more than just following recipes. It's about understanding the nuances of this innovative cooking method and making the most of your air fryer's capabilities. Here are some essential cooking tips to help you achieve culinary excellence:

1. Preheat Your Air Fryer: Just like with conventional ovens, preheating your air fryer is essential for consistent cooking results. Preheating ensures that your food starts cooking immediately when you place it in the basket.

2. Use the Right Amount of Oil: While air frying uses less oil than traditional frying methods, it's still important to use some oil for that crispy texture. Invest in an oil sprayer to apply a thin, even layer of oil to your food.

3. Don't Overcrowd the Basket: Overcrowding the basket can lead to uneven cooking. Make sure there's enough space for hot air to circulate around each piece of food. Cook in batches if necessary.

4. Shake and Toss: To ensure even cooking and browning, shake or toss your food in the basket midway through the cooking process. This simple step prevents sticking and promotes uniform results.

5. Experiment with Seasonings: Get creative with seasonings and marinades to add depth and flavor to your dishes. Herbs, spices, and sauces can transform ordinary recipes into extraordinary ones.

6. Check for Doneness: Invest in a reliable kitchen thermometer to check the internal temperature of meat and poultry. This ensures your dishes are cooked to perfection without guesswork.

7. Embrace Parchment Paper: To prevent food from sticking to the basket, consider using parchment paper. Just make sure it's properly secured to avoid interference with the fan.

8. Adjust Temperatures and Times: Every air fryer is slightly different, so don't be afraid to adjust temperatures and cooking times to suit your appliance. Keep an eye on your food the first few times you use it to get a feel for how it cooks.

9. Preparing Frozen Foods: Air fryers excel at cooking frozen foods like fries, chicken nuggets, and fish sticks. You can achieve a crispy exterior without thawing. Just add a few extra minutes to the cooking time.

10. Get Creative: Don't limit yourself to classic recipes. Use your air fryer to experiment with new dishes and ingredients. It's a versatile tool that can handle a wide range of culinary adventures.

11. Keep it Dry: Moisture is the enemy of crispiness. Pat food dry with paper towels before seasoning and cooking. This step is especially crucial for achieving crispy results.

12. Clean Regularly: A clean air fryer is essential for consistent performance. Follow the manufacturer's cleaning instructions and remove any food debris or excess oil after each use.

13. Use Accessories Wisely: Many air fryers come with accessories like racks and skewers. Experiment with these to expand your cooking possibilities, from grilling to baking.

14. Mind the Size: Pay attention to the size of your food items. Smaller pieces tend to cook faster, while larger items may need more time. Keep this in mind when planning your meals.

15. Keep an Eye on Delicate Items: Foods with delicate batters or coatings may require a light spray of oil to prevent sticking. It's a small step that can make a big difference in the final result.

By incorporating these cooking tips into your air frying repertoire, you'll be well on your way to creating culinary masterpieces that are not only delicious but also healthier than ever before.

AIR FRYER CLEANING AND MAINTENANCE

Maintaining your air fryer is essential to ensure its longevity and continued performance. Proper cleaning and care will keep your appliance in top shape, so you can enjoy countless crispy delights. Here's a comprehensive guide to air fryer cleaning and maintenance:

1. Unplug and Cool Down: Before cleaning your air fryer, always unplug it and allow it to cool down. Safety should be your top priority.

2. Disassemble for Cleaning: Most air fryers consist of several removable parts, such as the cooking basket, tray, and pan. Take these components apart to clean them thoroughly.

3. Hand Wash or Dishwasher: Check the manufacturer's instructions to determine if your air fryer accessories are dishwasher-safe. If they are, you can save time by placing them in the dishwasher. Otherwise, wash them by hand in warm, soapy water.

4. Be Gentle: Use a non-abrasive sponge or cloth to clean the interior and exterior of the air fryer. Scrubbing with abrasive materials can damage the non-stick coating.

5. Dealing with Stubborn Residue: If you encounter stubborn, stuck-on food residue, soak the affected parts in warm, soapy water for a few minutes to loosen it. Then, use a soft sponge to gently scrub it away.

6. Avoid Submerging Electronics: Never immerse the base of your air fryer in water or any liquid. This can damage the electrical components and pose a safety hazard.

7. Clean the Heating Element: Regularly inspect the heating element for any food particles or grease buildup. Use a soft brush or cloth to wipe it clean. Ensure the heating element is completely dry before reassembling the air fryer.

8. Empty the Crumb Tray: Many air fryers have a crumb tray or catch pan that collects food debris. Empty this tray after each use and clean it thoroughly to prevent smoke and odors during cooking.

9. Deodorize with Vinegar: If your air fryer retains odors from previous cooking sessions, try wiping the interior with a mixture of water and white vinegar. This can help neutralize unwanted smells.

10. Check the Seal: Inspect the seal around the cooking chamber for any damage or wear. A well-maintained seal ensures proper heat retention and even cooking.

11. Oil the Basket: Occasionally, apply a small amount of oil to the basket to prevent it from losing its non-stick properties. Use a paper towel to lightly coat the basket with oil.

12. Store Properly: When not in use, store your air fryer in a cool, dry place. Ensure it's protected from dust and humidity, which can affect its performance.

13. Regular Maintenance: Consider performing a deep clean every few weeks, depending on your usage. This involves disassembling the air fryer, cleaning all components, and checking for any signs of wear or malfunction.

14. Consult the Manual: Always consult your air fryer's user manual for specific cleaning and maintenance guidelines provided by the manufacturer.

By following these cleaning and maintenance practices, you'll not only extend the life of your air fryer but also ensure that each meal you prepare is as delicious and crispy as the last.

AIR FRYER HISTORY

The Fascinating Evolution of Air Frying: A Culinary Revolution

In the ever-evolving world of culinary technology, few innovations have captured the imagination of home cooks and food enthusiasts quite like the air fryer. This modern kitchen appliance has revolutionized the way we cook, offering a healthier alternative to traditional frying methods without sacrificing taste or texture. To truly appreciate the air fryer's place in our kitchens today, it's essential to delve into its intriguing history.

Early Beginnings: The Concept of Hot Air Cooking

The roots of the air fryer can be traced back to the idea of cooking with hot air, which has been explored by inventors and chefs for centuries. In the 18th century, French chef François Louis Boulanger experimented with hot air ovens, which used a hand-cranked fan to circulate heated air for baking and roasting. Although these early attempts were primitive compared to modern air fryers, they laid the foundation for the technology that would emerge much later.

The Microwave Oven Era: A Step Towards Air Frying

The microwave oven, which gained popularity in the mid-20th century, introduced a significant shift in cooking methods. Instead of relying on radiant heat, microwaves cooked food by emitting electromagnetic waves that agitated water molecules in the food, generating heat. While microwaves were revolutionary in their own right, they couldn't replicate the crispy texture and taste of deep-fried foods.

It was during the microwave oven era that some culinary enthusiasts began to explore the concept of combining hot air with microwave technology to achieve the desired crispiness. However, these early attempts remained largely experimental and were not yet ready for mainstream use.

The Advent of Convection Ovens: A Game-Changer

In the 1960s and 1970s, convection ovens made their debut in commercial kitchens. These ovens featured fans that circulated hot air around the food, resulting in faster and more even cooking. Convection ovens quickly gained popularity among professional chefs for their ability to roast, bake, and brown food more efficiently than traditional ovens.

The success of convection ovens in the culinary world sparked interest in developing smaller, more accessible versions for home use. This marked a significant step towards the creation of air fryers as we know them today. These early convection ovens offered a taste of what was possible, but they were still relatively bulky and expensive for the average consumer.

The Birth of the Air Fryer: Innovation Meets Convenience

The true turning point in the evolution of air frying came in the 21st century when inventors and engineers set out to create a more compact, user-friendly appliance that could mimic the results of deep frying without submerging food in oil. This marked the birth of the first-generation air fryer.

These early air fryers were designed to work on the principle of convection cooking. They featured a heating element and a high-powered fan that circulated hot air around the food. What set them apart from convection ovens was their compact size and user-friendly controls. These appliances were aimed squarely at home cooks who wanted a convenient way to prepare crispy, delicious dishes with minimal oil.

The Popularity Surge: A Healthier Way to Enjoy Fried Foods

The air fryer quickly gained popularity for its ability to produce crispy, golden-brown results with just a fraction of the oil used in traditional frying methods. Health-conscious individuals were particularly drawn to the air fryer's promise of reducing fat intake while retaining the flavors and textures they loved.

As word of mouth spread and more households embraced this innovative appliance, manufacturers began to refine their designs and add features to meet the growing demand. Digital controls, pre-programmed cooking settings, and a variety of accessories became common features, making air fryers even more versatile and user-friendly.

The Science Behind Air Frying: How It Works

To understand how air frying works, it's essential to delve into the science behind it. In an air fryer, the heating element heats the air inside the appliance to a high temperature. A powerful fan then circulates this hot air around the food, creating a convection current. This rapid circulation of hot air cooks the food from all angles, ensuring even cooking and browning.

What sets the air fryer apart from traditional deep frying is its minimal use of oil. While you can add a small amount of oil to enhance flavor and promote browning, it's not necessary for cooking. Instead, the hot air in the appliance crisps the food's outer layer, giving it a satisfying crunch without the excessive oil absorption associated with deep frying.

Air Fryer Versatility: Beyond Frying

While air fryers are known for their ability to produce crispy fried foods, their versatility extends far beyond frying. These appliances can bake, roast, grill, and even dehydrate a wide range of dishes. From perfectly cooked chicken wings and vegetable skewers to tender salmon fillets and homemade potato chips, the air fryer has become a staple in many kitchens due to its ability to handle a variety of cooking tasks.

The Evolution Continues: Advanced Features and Designs

As the popularity of air fryers continued to grow, manufacturers invested in research and development to improve their products. Second and third-generation air fryers emerged with enhanced features like touch-screen displays, smart technology compatibility, and larger cooking capacities.

Additionally, the design of air fryers evolved to accommodate various cooking needs. Some models now feature multiple cooking compartments, allowing users to prepare different dishes simultaneously without flavor transfer. This innovation further increased the appliance's appeal for busy households.

The Health Benefits of Air Frying

One of the key drivers behind the air fryer's success is its health-conscious appeal. By using significantly less oil than traditional frying methods, air frying reduces calorie and fat intake, making it a preferred choice for those looking to maintain a balanced diet. The absence of submersion in hot oil also means that air-fried foods contain fewer harmful compounds generated during deep frying, such as acrylamide.

Furthermore, air frying retains the nutritional value of foods better than deep frying. Vegetables, for example, maintain their vitamins and minerals when cooked in an air fryer, resulting in healthier and more nutritious meals.

The Air Fryer's Impact on Culinary Culture

The air fryer has had a profound impact on culinary culture around the world. It has influenced the way people approach cooking and meal preparation, making it easier for individuals to enjoy their favorite fried dishes without the guilt associated with excess oil consumption.

Moreover, the air fryer has encouraged culinary experimentation. Home cooks have embraced the challenge of adapting traditional recipes to air frying, resulting in innovative and healthier versions of classic dishes. From air-fried doughnuts to crispy tofu, the possibilities are endless.

The Future of Air Frying: A Bright Horizon

As we look to the future, it's clear that air frying has firmly established itself as a permanent fixture in the world of cooking appliances. Manufacturers are likely to continue refining and expanding their product lines, offering consumers even more advanced features and capabilities.

Furthermore, the health-conscious trend in modern cooking is unlikely to fade, which means that the demand for air fryers will remain strong. Innovations in cooking techniques and technologies may lead to further enhancements in air frying methods, making it an even more efficient and convenient way to prepare delicious and healthy meals.

The history of the air fryer is a testament to human ingenuity and our relentless pursuit of healthier, more convenient cooking methods. From the early experiments with hot air ovens to the birth of the modern air fryer, this culinary innovation has come a long way. It has not only changed the way we cook but also influenced our dietary choices and our approach to enjoying fried foods in a healthier manner.

As air fryers continue to evolve and improve, they are likely to become an even more integral part of our kitchens. Their versatility, convenience, and health benefits make them a valuable addition to any household. Whether you're a health-conscious individual looking to enjoy your favorite fried dishes guilt-free or a busy home cook seeking a quick and efficient way to prepare meals, the air fryer has something to offer.

In addition to their practical applications, air fryers have also sparked a sense of culinary creativity among home cooks and professional chefs alike. The challenge of adapting and experimenting with air frying techniques has led to a wide range of innovative recipes and unique twists on traditional favorites. This culinary exploration is a testament to the enduring appeal of the air fryer.

The air fryer's impact on culinary culture extends beyond just the appliance itself. It has contributed to a broader conversation about the importance of healthy eating and the role of technology in supporting our dietary choices. As consumers become more health-conscious and seek ways to maintain balanced diets, the air fryer serves as a symbol of how innovation can align with our desire for delicious, wholesome food.

In conclusion, the air fryer's fascinating history reflects our ongoing quest for better and healthier cooking methods. From early experiments with hot air to the development of sophisticated modern appliances, it has become a staple in kitchens worldwide. With its potential for continued innovation and its ability to cater to the demands of health-conscious consumers, the air fryer is poised to remain a culinary game-changer for years to come. Its journey from concept to kitchen countertop is a testament to the enduring human drive to improve our culinary experiences and make them both delicious and health-conscious.

COOKING MEASUREMENT CONVERSION CHART

Dry Measurements	
Measurement	**Equivalent**
1 pound	16 ounces
1 cup	16 tablespoons
3/4 cup	12 tablespoons
2/3 cup	10 tablespoons plus 2 teaspoons
1/2 cup	8 tablespoons
3/8 cup	6 tablespoons
1/3 cup	5 tablespoons plus 1 teaspoon
1/4 cup	4 tablespoons
1/6 cup	2 tablespoons plus 2 teaspoons
1/8 cup	2 tablespoons
1/16 cup	1 tablespoon
1 tablespoon	3 teaspoons
1/8 teaspoon	Pinch
1/16 teaspoon	Dash
1/2 cup butter	1 stick of butter

Liquid Measurements	
Measurement	**Equivalent (rounded for ease of use)**
4 quarts	1 gallon
2 quarts	1/2 gallon
1 quart	1/4 gallon
2 pints	1 quart
4 cups	1 quart
2 cups	1/2 quart
2 cups	1 pint
1 cup	1/2 pint
1 cup	1/4 quart
1 cup	8 fluid ounces
3/4 cup	6 fluid ounces
2/3 cup	5.3 fluid ounces
1/2 cup	4 fluid ounces
1/3 cup	2.7 fluid ounces
1/4 cup	2 fluid ounces
1 tablespoon	0.5 fluid ounces

U.S. to Metric Conversions

U.S. Measurement	Metric Conversion (rounded for ease of use)
Weight Measurements	
1 pound	454 grams
8 ounces	227 grams
4 ounces	113 grams
1 ounce	28 grams
Volume Measurements	
4 quarts	3.8 liters
4 cups (1 quart)	0.95 liters
2 cups	473 milliliters
1 cup	237 milliliters
3/4 cup	177 milliliters
2/3 cup	158 milliliters
1/2 cup	118 milliliters
1/3 cup	79 milliliters
1/4 cup	59 milliliters
1/5 cup	47 milliliters
1 tablespoon	15 milliliters
1 teaspoon	5 milliliters
1/2 teaspoon	2.5 milliliters
1/5 teaspoon	1 milliliter
Fluid Measurements	
34 fluid ounces	1 liter
8 fluid ounces	237 milliliters
3.4 fluid ounces	100 milliliters
1 fluid ounce	30 milliliters

Metric to U.S. Conversions	
Metric Measurement (rounded for ease of use)	**U.S. Conversion**
Weight Measurements	
500 grams	1.10 pounds
100 grams	3.5 ounces
50 grams	1.8 ounces
1 gram	0.04 ounces
Volume Measurements	
1 liter	0.26 gallons
1 liter	1.06 quarts
1 liter	2.1 pints
1 liter	4.2 cups
500 milliliters	2.1 cups
237 milliliters	1 cup
177 milliliters	3/4 cup
158 milliliters	2/3 cup
118 milliliters	1/2 cup
100 milliliters	2/5 cup
79 milliliters	1/3 cup
59 milliliters	1/4 cup
47 milliliters	1/5 cup
15 milliliters	1 tablespoon
5 milliliters	1 teaspoon
2.5 milliliters	1/2 teaspoon
1 milliliter	1/5 teaspoon
Fluid Measurements	
1 liter	34 fluid ounces
237 milliliters	8 fluid ounces
100 milliliters	3.4 fluid ounces
30 milliliters	1 fluid ounce

CRISPY POTATO HASH BROWNS

Prep time: 10 mins | **Cook time:** 15 mins | **Total time:** 25 mins | **Servings:** 4

Ingredients:

- 4 large potatoes, peeled and grated
- 1 onion, finely chopped
- 2 tbsp olive oil
- Salt and pepper to taste

Directions:

1. Preheat your air fryer to 180°C (360°F).

2. In a bowl, combine grated potatoes and chopped onions. Drizzle with olive oil and season with salt and pepper. Mix well.

3. Divide the mixture into equal portions and place them in the air fryer basket.

4. Cook for 15 minutes, flipping halfway through, until golden and crispy.

5. Serve hot with your favorite breakfast sides.

Nutrition Facts: (Per Serving)

- Calories: 180
- Fat: 7g
- Carbohydrates: 28g
- Protein: 3g

AIR-FRIED FRENCH TOAST STICKS

Prep time: 10 mins | **Cook time:** 8 mins | **Total time:** 18 mins | **Servings:** 4

Ingredients:

- 8 slices of bread, cut into sticks
- 2 eggs
- 1/2 cup milk
- 1 tsp vanilla extract
- 1/2 tsp ground cinnamon
- Maple syrup for dipping

Directions:

1. In a bowl, whisk together eggs, milk, vanilla extract, and ground cinnamon.
2. Dip each bread stick into the egg mixture, ensuring it's coated evenly.
3. Place the coated sticks in the air fryer basket, making sure they are not touching.
4. Cook at 180°C (360°F) for 8 minutes or until golden brown, flipping halfway through.
5. Serve with maple syrup for dipping.

Nutrition Facts: (Per Serving)

- Calories: 220
- Fat: 7g
- Carbohydrates: 31g
- Protein: 8g

VEGGIE OMELETTE IN THE AIR FRYER

Prep time: 10 mins | **Cook time:** 10 mins | **Total time:** 20 mins | **Servings:** 2

Ingredients:

- 4 eggs
- 1/4 cup bell peppers, diced
- 1/4 cup onions, diced
- 1/4 cup tomatoes, diced
- 1/4 cup grated cheese
- Salt and pepper to taste

Directions:

1. In a bowl, beat the eggs and add diced vegetables, grated cheese, salt, and pepper.
2. Pour the mixture into an air fryer-safe pan.
3. Preheat the air fryer to 180°C (360°F) and place the pan inside.
4. Cook for 10 minutes or until the omelette is set and slightly golden.
5. Slice and serve hot.

Nutrition Facts: (Per Serving)

- Calories: 230
- Fat: 16g
- Carbohydrates: 6g
- Protein: 15g

BANANA WALNUT MUFFINS

Prep time: 15 mins | **Cook time:** 15 mins | **Total time:** 30 mins | **Servings:** 6

Ingredients:

- 2 ripe bananas, mashed
- 1/4 cup melted butter
- 1/2 cup sugar
- 1 egg
- 1 tsp vanilla extract
- 1 1/2 cups self-raising flour
- 1/2 cup chopped walnuts

Directions:

1. In a bowl, mix mashed bananas, melted butter, sugar, egg, and vanilla extract.

2. Gradually add the self-raising flour and chopped walnuts, stirring until just combined.

3. Divide the batter into greased muffin cups.

4. Preheat the air fryer to 180°C (360°F) and place the muffin cups inside.

5. Cook for 15 minutes or until a toothpick comes out clean when inserted into a muffin.

Nutrition Facts: (Per Serving)

- Calories: 310
- Fat: 14g
- Carbohydrates: 42g
- Protein: 5g

AIR-FRIED BREAKFAST BURRITOS

Prep time: 15 mins | **Cook time:** 10 mins | **Total time:** 25 mins | **Servings:** 4

Ingredients:

- 4 large flour tortillas
- 4 eggs, scrambled
- 1/2 cup cooked bacon, crumbled
- 1/2 cup shredded cheddar cheese
- Salsa and sour cream for serving

Directions:

1. Lay out each tortilla and fill with scrambled eggs, crumbled bacon, and shredded cheese.

2. Fold in the sides of the tortilla and roll it up tightly.

3. Preheat the air fryer to 180°C (360°F) and place the burritos seam side down in the basket.

4. Cook for 10 minutes, turning halfway through, until golden and crispy.

5. Serve with salsa and sour cream.

Nutrition Facts: (Per Serving)

- Calories: 420
- Fat: 23g
- Carbohydrates: 28g
- Protein: 23g

CINNAMON SUGAR DONUT HOLES

Prep time: 15 mins | **Cook time:** 5 mins | **Total time:** 20 mins | **Servings:** 4

Ingredients:

- 1 cup self-raising flour
- 1/4 cup sugar
- 1/2 tsp ground cinnamon
- 1/2 cup milk
- 1/2 tsp vanilla extract
- 2 tbsp melted butter
- 1/4 cup powdered sugar

Directions:

1. In a bowl, combine self-raising flour, sugar, and ground cinnamon.

2. Stir in milk and vanilla extract to form a batter.

3. Roll the batter into small balls and place them in the air fryer basket.

4. Preheat the air fryer to 180°C (360°F) and cook for 5 minutes until golden brown.

5. While still warm, brush the donut holes with melted butter and roll in powdered sugar.

Nutrition Facts: (Per Serving)

- Calories: 260
- Fat: 6g
- Carbohydrates: 45g
- Protein: 4g

SMASHED AVOCADO TOAST

Prep time: 5 mins | **Cook time:** 5 mins | **Total time:** 10 mins | **Servings:** 2

Ingredients:

- 2 slices of wholemeal bread
- 1 ripe avocado
- Juice of 1/2 lemon
- Salt and pepper to taste
- Red pepper flakes for garnish (optional)

Directions:

1. Toast the slices of bread in the air fryer for 2-3 minutes until crispy.

2. While the bread is toasting, mash the ripe avocado in a bowl and add lemon juice, salt, and pepper.

3. Spread the mashed avocado over the toasted bread.

4. Return the avocado toast to the air fryer and cook for an additional 2-3 minutes until the avocado is warmed through.

5. Sprinkle with red pepper flakes if desired and serve.

Nutrition Facts: (Per Serving)

- Calories: 220
- Fat: 14g
- Carbohydrates: 21g
- Protein: 4g

BLUEBERRY PANCAKES

Prep time: 10 mins | **Cook time:** 10 mins | **Total time:** 20 mins | **Servings:** 4

Ingredients:

- 1 cup self-raising flour
- 1 tbsp sugar
- 1 egg
- 1 cup milk
- 1/2 cup fresh blueberries
- Butter for serving
- Maple syrup for drizzling

Directions:

1. In a bowl, combine self-raising flour and sugar.

2. In another bowl, whisk together the egg and milk.

3. Pour the wet ingredients into the dry ingredients and stir until just combined.

4. Gently fold in the fresh blueberries.

5. Preheat the air fryer to 180°C (360°F) and lightly grease the basket.

6. Pour 1/4 cup of batter for each pancake into the air fryer and cook for 5 minutes on each side until golden brown.

7. Serve with butter and drizzle with maple syrup.

Nutrition Facts: (Per Serving)

- Calories: 250
- Fat: 6g
- Carbohydrates: 42g
- Protein: 7g

SAUSAGE AND EGG BREAKFAST BURRITOS

Prep time: 15 mins | **Cook time:** 10 mins | **Total time:** 25 mins | **Servings:** 4

Ingredients:

- 4 large flour tortillas
- 8 cooked breakfast sausages
- 4 eggs, scrambled
- 1/2 cup shredded cheddar cheese
- Salt and pepper to taste
- Salsa for serving

Directions:

1. Lay out each tortilla and fill with scrambled eggs, sausages, shredded cheese, salt, and pepper.

2. Fold in the sides of the tortilla and roll it up tightly.

3. Preheat the air fryer to 180°C (360°F) and place the burritos seam side down in the basket.

4. Cook for 10 minutes, turning halfway through, until golden and crispy.

5. Serve with salsa.

Nutrition Facts: (Per Serving)

- Calories: 450
- Fat: 28g
- Carbohydrates: 24g
- Protein: 25g

VEGGIE BREAKFAST QUESADILLAS

Prep time: 10 mins | **Cook time:** 10 mins | **Total time:** 20 mins | **Servings:** 2

Ingredients:

- 4 small wholemeal tortillas
- 1/2 cup grated cheddar cheese
- 1/2 cup bell peppers, diced
- 1/4 cup onions, diced
- 1/4 cup mushrooms, sliced
- 1/4 cup spinach leaves
- Salt and pepper to taste

Directions:

1. Lay out two tortillas and sprinkle each with half of the grated cheddar cheese.
2. Distribute the diced bell peppers, onions, mushrooms, and spinach evenly over the cheese.
3. Season with salt and pepper.
4. Top each with a second tortilla to create a quesadilla.
5. Preheat the air fryer to 180°C (360°F) and place the quesadillas inside.
6. Cook for 5-7 minutes on each side until the tortillas are crisp and the cheese is melted.
7. Slice into wedges and serve.

Nutrition Facts: (Per Serving)

- Calories: 320
- Fat: 15g
- Carbohydrates: 38g
- Protein: 15g

LUNCH

AIR-FRIED CHICKEN TENDERS

Prep time: 15 mins | **Cook time:** 12 mins | **Total time:** 27 mins | **Servings:** 4

Ingredients:

- 1 pound chicken tenders
- 1 cup breadcrumbs
- 1/2 cup grated Parmesan cheese
- 1 tsp paprika
- 1/2 tsp garlic powder
- Salt and pepper to taste
- Cooking spray

Directions:

1. In a bowl, combine breadcrumbs, Parmesan cheese, paprika, garlic powder, salt, and pepper.

2. Coat each chicken tender with the breadcrumb mixture, pressing the coating onto the chicken.

3. Preheat the air fryer to 200°C (390°F) and lightly grease the basket with cooking spray.

4. Place the chicken tenders in the basket without overcrowding.

5. Cook for 12 minutes, flipping halfway through, until the chicken is crispy and cooked through.

6. Serve with your favorite dipping sauces.

Nutrition Facts: (Per Serving)

- Calories: 320
- Fat: 9g
- Carbohydrates: 22g
- Protein: 35g

MEDITERRANEAN QUINOA SALAD

Prep time: 15 mins | **Cook time:** 12 mins | **Total time:** 27 mins | **Servings:** 4

Ingredients:

- 1 cup quinoa, rinsed and drained
- 2 cups water
- 1/2 cucumber, diced
- 1/2 cup cherry tomatoes, halved
- 1/4 cup red onion, finely chopped
- 1/4 cup Kalamata olives, pitted and sliced
- 1/4 cup crumbled feta cheese
- 2 tbsp olive oil
- 1 tbsp lemon juice
- 1 tsp dried oregano
- Salt and pepper to taste

Directions:

1. In a saucepan, bring 2 cups of water to a boil. Add quinoa and reduce heat to low. Cover and simmer for 12 minutes or until quinoa is cooked and water is absorbed.

2. Fluff the cooked quinoa with a fork and let it cool.

3. In a large bowl, combine quinoa, cucumber, cherry tomatoes, red onion, Kalamata olives, and feta cheese.

4. In a small bowl, whisk together olive oil, lemon juice, dried oregano, salt, and pepper.

5. Drizzle the dressing over the salad and toss to combine.

6. Serve as a refreshing and healthy lunch option.

Nutrition Facts: (Per Serving)

- Calories: 320
- Fat: 15g
- Carbohydrates: 38g
- Protein: 15g

CRISPY TOFU AND VEGETABLE STIR-FRY

Prep time: 20 mins | **Cook time:** 15 mins | **Total time:** 35 mins | **Servings:** 4

Ingredients:

- 1 block firm tofu, cubed
- 2 tbsp soy sauce
- 1 tbsp cornstarch
- 2 tbsp vegetable oil
- 1 red bell pepper, sliced
- 1 yellow bell pepper, sliced
- 1 cup broccoli florets
- 1 cup snap peas
- 1/4 cup hoisin sauce
- 2 tbsp sesame seeds
- Cooked rice for serving

Directions:

1. In a bowl, combine cubed tofu, soy sauce, and cornstarch. Toss to coat the tofu evenly.

2. Preheat the air fryer to 200°C (390°F) and lightly grease the basket with vegetable oil.

3. Place the tofu in the air fryer basket and cook for 15 minutes, shaking the basket occasionally until the tofu is crispy.

4. While the tofu is cooking, heat 1 tablespoon of vegetable oil in a pan over medium heat.

5. Stir-fry the sliced bell peppers, broccoli, and snap peas for 5-7 minutes until they are tender.

6. Add the crispy tofu to the stir-fried vegetables and pour hoisin sauce over the mixture. Stir to coat everything evenly.

7. Serve the tofu and vegetable stir-fry over cooked rice and garnish with sesame seeds.

Nutrition Facts: (Per Serving)

- Calories: 350
- Fat: 16g
- Carbohydrates: 36g
- Protein: 18g

AIR-FRIED FALAFEL

Prep time: 15 mins | **Cook time:** 12 mins | **Total time:** 27 mins | **Servings:** 4

Ingredients:

- 1 can (400g) chickpeas, drained and rinsed
- 1/4 cup fresh parsley, chopped
- 1/4 cup red onion, chopped
- 2 cloves garlic, minced
- 1 tsp ground cumin
- 1 tsp ground coriander
- 1/2 tsp baking powder
- Salt and pepper to taste
- Cooking spray

Directions:

1. In a food processor, combine chickpeas, parsley, red onion, garlic, ground cumin, ground coriander, baking powder, salt, and pepper.
2. Pulse until the mixture becomes a coarse paste.
3. Form the mixture into small falafel patties.
4. Preheat the air fryer to 200°C (390°F) and lightly grease the basket with cooking spray.
5. Place the falafel patties in the basket, making sure they are not overcrowded.
6. Cook for 12 minutes, turning halfway through, until the falafel is crispy and cooked through.
7. Serve with pita bread and tahini sauce.

Nutrition Facts: (Per Serving)

- Calories: 220
- Fat: 5g
- Carbohydrates: 35g
- Protein: 10g

CAPRESE PANINI WITH PESTO

Prep time: 10 mins | **Cook time:** 5 mins | **Total time:** 15 mins | **Servings:** 2

Ingredients:

- 4 slices of ciabatta bread
- 2 tbsp pesto sauce
- 4 slices of mozzarella cheese
- 1 large tomato, sliced
- Fresh basil leaves
- Olive oil for brushing

Directions:

1. Spread pesto sauce on two slices of ciabatta bread.
2. Layer mozzarella cheese, tomato slices, and fresh basil leaves on top of the pesto.
3. Place the remaining two slices of ciabatta bread on top to form sandwiches.
4. Brush the outsides of the sandwiches with olive oil.
5. Preheat the air fryer to 180°C (360°F) and place the sandwiches inside.
6. Cook for 5 minutes until the bread is crispy, and the cheese is melted.
7. Slice and serve your Caprese panini with a side salad.

Nutrition Facts: (Per Serving)

- Calories: 420
- Fat: 20g
- Carbohydrates: 42g
- Protein: 18g

SPINACH AND MUSHROOM STUFFED CHICKEN BREAST

Prep time: 20 mins | **Cook time:** 25 mins | **Total time:** 45 mins | **Servings:** 4

Ingredients:

- 4 boneless, skinless chicken breasts
- 1 cup fresh spinach leaves
- 1/2 cup mushrooms, sliced
- 1/2 cup feta cheese, crumbled
- 1 tsp olive oil
- 1 tsp Italian seasoning
- Salt and pepper to taste
- Toothpicks for securing

Directions:

1. Preheat the air fryer to 180°C (360°F).

2. In a pan, heat olive oil over medium heat and sauté mushrooms until they release their moisture and turn golden brown.

3. Remove from heat and let cool.

4. Slice a pocket into each chicken breast, being careful not to cut all the way through.

5. Stuff each chicken breast with fresh spinach, sautéed mushrooms, and crumbled feta cheese.

6. Secure the pockets with toothpicks.

7. Season the chicken breasts with Italian seasoning, salt, and pepper.

8. Place the stuffed chicken breasts in the air fryer basket.

9. Cook for 25 minutes, flipping halfway through, until the chicken is cooked through and the cheese is melted.

10. Remove the toothpicks before serving.

Nutrition Facts: (Per Serving)

- Calories: 290
- Fat: 13g
- Carbohydrates: 2g
- Protein: 40g

AIR-FRIED BEEF AND VEGETABLE SKEWERS

Prep time: 20 mins | **Cook time:** 15 mins | **Total time:** 35 mins | **Servings:** 4

Ingredients:

- 1 pound beef sirloin, cut into cubes
- 1 red bell pepper, cut into chunks
- 1 yellow bell pepper, cut into chunks
- 1 red onion, cut into chunks
- 1 zucchini, sliced
- 2 tbsp olive oil
- 1 tsp garlic powder
- 1 tsp paprika
- Salt and pepper to taste
- Wooden skewers, soaked in water

Directions:

1. In a bowl, combine beef sirloin cubes with olive oil, garlic powder, paprika, salt, and pepper. Toss to coat.
2. Thread the marinated beef, red bell pepper, yellow bell pepper, red onion, and zucchini onto wooden skewers.
3. Preheat the air fryer to 200°C (390°F).
4. Place the skewers in the air fryer basket, ensuring they are not overcrowded.
5. Cook for 15 minutes, turning the skewers halfway through, until the beef is cooked to your desired level of doneness.
6. Serve the beef and vegetable skewers with rice or a side salad.

Nutrition Facts: (Per Serving)

- Calories: 320
- Fat: 18g
- Carbohydrates: 8g
- Protein: 32g

AIR-FRIED CHICKEN QUESADILLAS

Prep time: 15 mins | **Cook time:** 10 mins | **Total time:** 25 mins | **Servings:** 4

Ingredients:

- 4 large flour tortillas
- 2 cups cooked chicken, shredded
- 1 cup shredded cheddar cheese
- 1/2 cup diced tomatoes
- 1/4 cup diced red onion
- 1/4 cup chopped cilantro
- 1/4 cup sour cream for serving
- Salsa for serving

Directions:

1. Lay out each tortilla and sprinkle with shredded cheddar cheese.

2. Distribute the cooked chicken, diced tomatoes, diced red onion, and chopped cilantro evenly over the cheese.

3. Top each with a second tortilla to create a quesadilla.

4. Preheat the air fryer to 180°C (360°F) and lightly grease the basket.

5. Place the quesadillas in the air fryer, one at a time, and cook for 5 minutes on each side until they are crispy and the cheese is melted.

6. Slice into wedges and serve with sour cream and salsa.

Nutrition Facts: (Per Serving)

- Calories: 450
- Fat: 18g
- Carbohydrates: 38g
- Protein: 30g

AIR-FRIED VEGGIE SPRING ROLLS

Prep time: 30 mins | **Cook time:** 10 mins | **Total time:** 40 mins | **Servings:** 4

Ingredients:

- 8 spring roll wrappers
- 2 cups shredded cabbage
- 1 cup shredded carrots
- 1 cup bean sprouts
- 1/4 cup chopped fresh cilantro
- 1/4 cup chopped fresh mint
- 1/4 cup chopped fresh basil
- 1/4 cup soy sauce
- 1/4 cup rice vinegar
- 1 tsp sesame oil
- 1 tsp honey
- Cooking spray

Directions:

1. In a large bowl, combine shredded cabbage, shredded carrots, bean sprouts, cilantro, mint, and basil.

2. In a small bowl, whisk together soy sauce, rice vinegar, sesame oil, and honey to make the dipping sauce.

3. Lay out a spring roll wrapper and place a portion of the vegetable mixture in the center.

4. Fold in the sides of the wrapper and roll it up tightly, sealing the edges with a bit of water.

5. Preheat the air fryer to 180°C (360°F) and lightly grease the basket with cooking spray.

6. Place the spring rolls in the air fryer, making sure they are not touching.

7. Cook for 10 minutes, turning halfway through, until the spring rolls are golden and crispy.

8. Serve with the dipping sauce.

Nutrition Facts: (Per Serving)

- Calories: 220
- Fat: 2g
- Carbohydrates: 45g
- Protein: 5g

APPETIZERS AND SNACKS

AIR-FRIED MOZZARELLA STICKS

Prep time: 15 mins | **Cook time:** 10 mins | **Total time:** 25 mins | **Servings:** 4

Ingredients:

- 12 mozzarella sticks
- 1 cup breadcrumbs
- 1/2 cup grated Parmesan cheese
- 1 tsp Italian seasoning
- 2 eggs, beaten
- Marinara sauce for dipping

Directions:

1. In a bowl, combine breadcrumbs, grated Parmesan cheese, and Italian seasoning.

2. Dip each mozzarella stick into beaten eggs, then coat with the breadcrumb mixture, pressing the coating onto the sticks.

3. Preheat the air fryer to 200°C (390°F) and lightly grease the basket.

4. Place the mozzarella sticks in the basket, ensuring they are not overcrowded.

5. Cook for 10 minutes until the mozzarella sticks are crispy and the cheese is melted.

6. Serve hot with marinara sauce for dipping.

Nutrition Facts: (Per Serving)

- Calories: 320
- Fat: 14g
- Carbohydrates: 25g
- Protein: 20g

AIR-FRIED BUFFALO CAULIFLOWER BITES

Prep time: 15 mins | **Cook time:** 15 mins | **Total time:** 30 mins | **Servings:** 4

Ingredients:

- 1 head cauliflower, cut into florets
- 1 cup breadcrumbs
- 1/2 cup all-purpose flour
- 1 tsp garlic powder
- 1 tsp paprika
- Salt and pepper to taste
- 1/2 cup buffalo sauce
- 2 tbsp melted butter
- Ranch dressing for dipping

Directions:

1. In a bowl, combine breadcrumbs, all-purpose flour, garlic powder, paprika, salt, and pepper.

2. Dip each cauliflower floret into water and then coat with the breadcrumb mixture, pressing the coating onto the florets.

3. Preheat the air fryer to 200°C (390°F) and lightly grease the basket.

4. Place the cauliflower florets in the basket, ensuring they are not overcrowded.

5. Cook for 15 minutes until the cauliflower bites are crispy.

6. In a separate bowl, mix buffalo sauce and melted butter.

7. Toss the cooked cauliflower bites in the buffalo sauce mixture.

8. Serve with ranch dressing for dipping.

Nutrition Facts: (Per Serving)

- Calories: 220
- Fat: 7g
- Carbohydrates: 34g
- Protein: 8g

AIR-FRIED JALAPEÑO POPPERS

Prep time: 20 mins | **Cook time:** 10 mins | **Total time:** 30 mins | **Servings:** 4

Ingredients:

- 12 fresh jalapeño peppers
- 8 oz cream cheese, softened
- 1 cup shredded cheddar cheese
- 1/2 cup breadcrumbs
- 1/2 cup bacon bits
- Cooking spray
- Ranch dressing for dipping

Directions:

1. Cut the tops off the jalapeño peppers and remove the seeds and membranes.

2. In a bowl, mix cream cheese, shredded cheddar cheese, and bacon bits.

3. Fill each jalapeño pepper with the cream cheese mixture.

4. Preheat the air fryer to 180°C (360°F) and lightly grease the basket with cooking spray.

5. Place the stuffed jalapeño peppers in the basket, ensuring they are not touching.

6. Cook for 10 minutes until the peppers are tender and the filling is melted and bubbly.

7. Serve with ranch dressing for dipping.

Nutrition Facts: (Per Serving)

- Calories: 320
- Fat: 24g
- Carbohydrates: 13g
- Protein: 13g

AIR-FRIED ONION RINGS

Prep time: 15 mins | **Cook time:** 10 mins | **Total time:** 25 mins | **Servings:** 4

Ingredients:

- 2 large onions, cut into rings
- 1 cup breadcrumbs
- 1/2 cup all-purpose flour
- 1 tsp paprika
- 1/2 tsp garlic powder
- Salt and pepper to taste
- 2 eggs, beaten
- Cooking spray
- Ketchup for dipping

Directions:

1. In a bowl, combine breadcrumbs, all-purpose flour, paprika, garlic powder, salt, and pepper.

2. Dip each onion ring into beaten eggs, then coat with the breadcrumb mixture, pressing the coating onto the rings.

3. Preheat the air fryer to 200°C (390°F) and lightly grease the basket with cooking spray.

4. Place the onion rings in the basket, ensuring they are not overcrowded.

5. Cook for 10 minutes until the onion rings are crispy and golden.

6. Serve hot with ketchup for dipping.

Nutrition Facts: (Per Serving)

- Calories: 220
- Fat: 6g
- Carbohydrates: 38g
- Protein: 6g

AIR-FRIED MINI MEATBALLS

Prep time: 20 mins | **Cook time:** 15 mins | **Total time:** 35 mins | **Servings:** 4

Ingredients:

- 1/2 pound ground beef
- 1/2 pound ground pork
- 1/4 cup breadcrumbs
- 1/4 cup grated Parmesan cheese
- 1/4 cup milk
- 1/4 cup chopped parsley
- 1 egg
- 1/2 tsp garlic powder
- 1/2 tsp dried oregano
- Salt and pepper to taste
- Marinara sauce for dipping

Directions:

1. In a bowl, combine ground beef, ground pork, breadcrumbs, grated Parmesan cheese, milk, chopped parsley, egg, garlic powder, dried oregano, salt, and pepper.

2. Form the mixture into mini meatballs.

3. Preheat the air fryer to 180°C (360°F) and lightly grease the basket with cooking spray.

4. Place the mini meatballs in the basket, ensuring they are not overcrowded.

5. Cook for 15 minutes, turning halfway through, until the meatballs are cooked through and browned.

6. Serve with marinara sauce for dipping.

Nutrition Facts: (Per Serving)

- Calories: 320
- Fat: 21g
- Carbohydrates: 7g
- Protein: 25g

AIR-FRIED AVOCADO FRIES

Prep time: 15 mins | **Cook time:** 10 mins | **Total time:** 25 mins | **Servings:** 4

Ingredients:

- 2 ripe avocados, sliced into strips
- 1 cup breadcrumbs
- 1/2 cup all-purpose flour
- 1 tsp paprika
- 1/2 tsp garlic powder
- Salt and pepper to taste
- 2 eggs, beaten
- Cooking spray
- Ranch dressing for dipping

Directions:

1. In a bowl, combine breadcrumbs, all-purpose flour, paprika, garlic powder, salt, and pepper.

2. Dip each avocado strip into beaten eggs, then coat with the breadcrumb mixture, pressing the coating onto the strips.

3. Preheat the air fryer to 200°C (390°F) and lightly grease the basket with cooking spray.

4. Place the avocado strips in the basket, ensuring they are not overcrowded.

5. Cook for 10 minutes until the avocado fries are crispy and golden.

6. Serve hot with ranch dressing for dipping.

Nutrition Facts: (Per Serving)

- Calories: 240
- Fat: 14g
- Carbohydrates: 25g
- Protein: 6g

AIR-FRIED STUFFED MUSHROOMS

Prep time: 20 mins | **Cook time:** 15 mins | **Total time:** 35 mins | **Servings:** 4

Ingredients:

- 16 large mushrooms, stems removed and reserved
- 1/2 cup breadcrumbs
- 1/4 cup grated Parmesan cheese
- 2 cloves garlic, minced
- 1/4 cup chopped fresh parsley
- 2 tbsp olive oil
- Salt and pepper to taste
- Cooking spray

Directions:

1. Finely chop the reserved mushroom stems.

2. In a bowl, combine chopped mushroom stems, breadcrumbs, grated Parmesan cheese, minced garlic, chopped fresh parsley, olive oil, salt, and pepper.

3. Fill each mushroom cap with the breadcrumb mixture.

4. Preheat the air fryer to 180°C (360°F) and lightly grease the basket with cooking spray.

5. Place the stuffed mushrooms in the basket, ensuring they are not overcrowded.

6. Cook for 15 minutes until the mushrooms are tender and the filling is golden brown.

7. Serve as a delicious appetizer.

Nutrition Facts: (Per Serving)

- Calories: 140
- Fat: 9g
- Carbohydrates: 12g
- Protein: 5g

AIR-FRIED SPINACH AND CHEESE PUFFS

Prep time: 20 mins | **Cook time:** 10 mins | **Total time:** 30 mins | **Servings:** 4

Ingredients:

- 1 sheet puff pastry, thawed
- 1 cup cooked spinach, squeezed dry and chopped
- 1 cup grated Gruyère cheese
- 1/4 cup grated Parmesan cheese
- 1/4 cup ricotta cheese
- 1 egg, beaten
- 1 tsp garlic powder
- Salt and pepper to taste
- Cooking spray

Directions:

1. Preheat the air fryer to 180°C (360°F).

2. In a bowl, combine cooked spinach, grated Gruyère cheese, grated Parmesan cheese, ricotta cheese, beaten egg, garlic powder, salt, and pepper.

3. Cut the puff pastry into small squares.

4. Place a spoonful of the spinach and cheese mixture in the center of each puff pastry square.

5. Fold the squares in half to form triangles and press the edges to seal.

6. Lightly grease the air fryer basket with cooking spray and place the spinach and cheese puffs inside.

7. Cook for 10 minutes until the puffs are golden brown and puffed up.

8. Serve as a delightful snack or appetizer.

Nutrition Facts: (Per Serving)

- Calories: 280
- Fat: 19g
- Carbohydrates: 18g
- Protein: 10g

AIR-FRIED COCONUT SHRIMP

Prep time: 20 mins | **Cook time:** 10 mins | **Total time:** 30 mins | **Servings:** 4

Ingredients:

- 12 large shrimp, peeled and deveined
- 1/2 cup shredded coconut
- 1/2 cup breadcrumbs
- 1/2 tsp paprika
- 1/4 tsp cayenne pepper
- Salt and pepper to taste
- 1 egg, beaten
- Cooking spray
- Sweet chili sauce for dipping

Directions:

1. In a bowl, combine shredded coconut, breadcrumbs, paprika, cayenne pepper, salt, and pepper.

2. Dip each shrimp into beaten egg, then coat with the breadcrumb mixture, pressing the coating onto the shrimp.

3. Preheat the air fryer to 200°C (390°F) and lightly grease the basket with cooking spray.

4. Place the coconut shrimp in the basket, ensuring they are not overcrowded.

5. Cook for 10 minutes until the shrimp are crispy and the coconut is toasted.

6. Serve hot with sweet chili sauce for dipping.

Nutrition Facts: (Per Serving)

- Calories: 240
- Fat: 12g
- Carbohydrates: 16g
- Protein: 15g

AIR-FRIED STUFFED JALAPEÑO POPPERS

Prep time: 20 mins | **Cook time:** 10 mins | **Total time:** 30 mins | **Servings:** 4

Ingredients:

- 12 fresh jalapeño peppers
- 4 oz cream cheese, softened
- 1/2 cup shredded cheddar cheese
- 1/4 cup cooked bacon bits
- Cooking spray
- Ranch dressing for dipping

Directions:

1. Cut the tops off the jalapeño peppers and remove the seeds and membranes.
2. In a bowl, mix cream cheese, shredded cheddar cheese, and cooked bacon bits.
3. Fill each jalapeño pepper with the cream cheese mixture.
4. Preheat the air fryer to 180°C (360°F) and lightly grease the basket with cooking spray.
5. Place the stuffed jalapeño peppers in the basket, ensuring they are not touching.
6. Cook for 10 minutes until the peppers are tender and the filling is melted and bubbly.
7. Serve with ranch dressing for dipping.

Nutrition Facts: (Per Serving)

- Calories: 280
- Fat: 24g
- Carbohydrates: 7g
- Protein: 10g

DINNER

AIR-FRIED LEMON HERB CHICKEN

Prep time: 15 mins | **Cook time:** 20 mins | **Total time:** 35 mins | **Servings:** 4

Ingredients:

- 4 boneless, skinless chicken breasts
- Zest and juice of 1 lemon
- 2 tbsp olive oil
- 2 cloves garlic, minced
- 1 tsp dried oregano
- 1 tsp dried thyme
- Salt and pepper to taste

Directions:

1. In a bowl, combine lemon zest, lemon juice, olive oil, minced garlic, dried oregano, dried thyme, salt, and pepper.

2. Place the chicken breasts in a resealable plastic bag and pour the lemon herb marinade over them.

3. Seal the bag and marinate in the refrigerator for at least 15 minutes.

4. Preheat the air fryer to 180°C (360°F) and lightly grease the basket.

5. Remove the chicken breasts from the marinade and place them in the air fryer basket.

6. Cook for 20 minutes, turning halfway through, until the chicken is cooked through and juices run clear.

7. Serve the lemon herb chicken with your choice of side dishes.

Nutrition Facts: (Per Serving)

- Calories: 240
- Fat: 10g
- Carbohydrates: 2g
- Protein: 35g

AIR-FRIED PORK CHOPS

Prep time: 15 mins | **Cook time:** 15 mins | **Total time:** 30 mins | **Servings:** 4

Ingredients:

- 4 pork chops
- 2 tbsp olive oil
- 1 tsp paprika
- 1 tsp garlic powder
- 1 tsp dried rosemary
- Salt and pepper to taste

Directions:

1. In a bowl, combine olive oil, paprika, garlic powder, dried rosemary, salt, and pepper.

2. Brush both sides of the pork chops with the olive oil mixture.

3. Preheat the air fryer to 200°C (390°F) and lightly grease the basket.

4. Place the pork chops in the basket, ensuring they are not overcrowded.

5. Cook for 15 minutes, turning halfway through, until the pork chops are cooked to your desired level of doneness.

6. Serve the air-fried pork chops with your favorite sides.

Nutrition Facts: (Per Serving)

- Calories: 280
- Fat: 15g
- Carbohydrates: 1g
- Protein: 35g

AIR-FRIED BBQ RIBS

Prep time: 20 mins | **Cook time:** 45 mins | **Total time:** 1 hr 5 mins | **Servings:** 4

Ingredients:

- 2 racks of baby back ribs
- 1 cup BBQ sauce
- 2 tbsp olive oil
- 1 tsp garlic powder
- 1 tsp paprika
- Salt and pepper to taste

Directions:

1. Remove the membrane from the back of the ribs and cut the racks into smaller sections.

2. In a bowl, combine olive oil, garlic powder, paprika, salt, and pepper.

3. Brush both sides of the ribs with the olive oil mixture.

4. Preheat the air fryer to 180°C (360°F) and lightly grease the basket.

5. Place the ribs in the basket, ensuring they are not overlapping.

6. Cook for 45 minutes, turning and basting with BBQ sauce every 15 minutes, until the ribs are tender and caramelized.

7. Serve the BBQ ribs with extra BBQ sauce for dipping.

Nutrition Facts: (Per Serving)

- Calories: 620
- Fat: 39g
- Carbohydrates: 22g
- Protein: 45g

AIR-FRIED VEGETARIAN STUFFED BELL PEPPERS

Prep time: 20 mins | **Cook time:** 30 mins | **Total time:** 50 mins | **Servings:** 4

Ingredients:

- 4 large bell peppers
- 1 cup cooked quinoa
- 1 cup black beans, drained and rinsed
- 1 cup corn kernels
- 1 cup diced tomatoes
- 1/2 cup shredded cheddar cheese
- 1 tsp chili powder
- Salt and pepper to taste
- Cooking spray

Directions:

1. Cut the tops off the bell peppers and remove the seeds and membranes.

2. In a bowl, combine cooked quinoa, black beans, corn kernels, diced tomatoes, shredded cheddar cheese, chili powder, salt, and pepper.

3. Stuff each bell pepper with the quinoa mixture.

4. Preheat the air fryer to 180°C (360°F) and lightly grease the basket with cooking spray.

5. Place the stuffed bell peppers in the basket, ensuring they are not overcrowded.

6. Cook for 30 minutes until the peppers are tender and the filling is heated through.

7. Serve as a delicious vegetarian dinner.

Nutrition Facts: (Per Serving)

- Calories: 350
- Fat: 8g
- Carbohydrates: 57g
- Protein: 13g

AIR-FRIED BEEF AND BROCCOLI

Prep time: 15 mins | **Cook time:** 15 mins | **Total time:** 30 mins | **Servings:** 4

Ingredients:

- 1 pound beef sirloin, thinly sliced
- 2 cups broccoli florets
- 1/4 cup soy sauce
- 2 tbsp brown sugar
- 1 tsp minced garlic
- 1 tsp minced ginger
- 1 tsp cornstarch
- 1 tsp sesame oil
- Cooking spray
- Cooked rice for serving

Directions:

1. In a bowl, whisk together soy sauce, brown sugar, minced garlic, minced ginger, cornstarch, and sesame oil to make the sauce.

2. Preheat the air fryer to 200°C (390°F).

3. Lightly grease the air fryer basket with cooking spray and place the sliced beef in a single layer.

4. Cook for 5 minutes, turning halfway through, until the beef is browned and cooked.

5. Remove the beef from the air fryer and set aside.

6. Place broccoli florets in the air fryer basket and cook for 5 minutes until they are tender-crisp.

7. Return the cooked beef to the air fryer and pour the sauce over the beef and broccoli.

8. Cook for an additional 5 minutes until the sauce thickens and coats the beef and broccoli.

9. Serve the beef and broccoli over cooked rice.

Nutrition Facts: (Per Serving)

- Calories: 340
- Fat: 12g
- Carbohydrates: 24g
- Protein: 32g

AIR-FRIED MUSHROOM RISOTTO

Prep time: 15 mins | **Cook time:** 30 mins | **Total time:** 45 mins | **Servings:** 4

Ingredients:

- 1 cup Arborio rice
- 8 oz mushrooms, sliced
- 1/2 cup diced onion
- 2 cloves garlic, minced
- 4 cups vegetable broth, heated
- 1/2 cup dry white wine
- 2 tbsp olive oil
- 1/4 cup grated Parmesan cheese
- Salt and pepper to taste
- Chopped fresh parsley for garnish

Directions:

1. In a pan, heat olive oil over medium heat and sauté mushrooms until they release their moisture and turn golden brown. Remove from the pan and set aside.

2. In the same pan, sauté diced onion and minced garlic until translucent.

3. Add Arborio rice and cook for 2 minutes, stirring constantly.

4. Pour in the dry white wine and cook until it's mostly absorbed.

5. Transfer the rice mixture to the air fryer basket.

6. Add the sautéed mushrooms and 1 cup of heated vegetable broth to the air fryer.

7. Cook at 180°C (360°F) for 15 minutes, stirring occasionally and adding more broth as needed until the rice is creamy and cooked.

8. Stir in grated Parmesan cheese and season with salt and pepper.

9. Garnish with chopped fresh parsley before serving.

Nutrition Facts: (Per Serving)

- Calories: 340
- Fat: 8g
- Carbohydrates: 53g
- Protein: 6g

AIR-FRIED COCONUT CURRY CHICKEN

Prep time: 15 mins | **Cook time:** 20 mins | **Total time:** 35 mins | **Servings:** 4

Ingredients:

- 4 boneless, skinless chicken breasts
- 1 can (400ml) coconut milk
- 2 tbsp red curry paste
- 1 cup sliced bell peppers
- 1 cup sliced zucchini
- 1 cup sliced carrots
- 1 cup sliced onions
- 2 tbsp vegetable oil
- Salt and pepper to taste
- Cooked rice for serving

Directions:

1. In a bowl, whisk together coconut milk and red curry paste to make the sauce.

2. Preheat the air fryer to 200°C (390°F).

3. Lightly grease the air fryer basket with vegetable oil and place the chicken breasts in a single layer.

4. Cook for 10 minutes, turning halfway through, until the chicken is browned and cooked.

5. Remove the chicken from the air fryer and slice it into strips.

6. In the same pan, sauté sliced bell peppers, zucchini, carrots, and onions in vegetable oil until they are tender-crisp.

7. Return the sliced chicken to the pan and pour the coconut curry sauce over the mixture.

8. Cook for an additional 5 minutes until the sauce is heated through and the chicken and vegetables are coated.

9. Serve the coconut curry chicken over cooked rice.

Nutrition Facts: (Per Serving)

- Calories: 420
- Fat: 22g
- Carbohydrates: 22g
- Protein: 35g

AIR-FRIED TOFU AND VEGETABLE STIR-FRY

Prep time: 20 mins | **Cook time:** 15 mins | **Total time:** 35 mins | **Servings:** 4

Ingredients:

- 1 block (400g) firm tofu, cubed
- 2 tbsp soy sauce
- 1 tbsp cornstarch
- 2 tbsp vegetable oil
- 1 cup sliced bell peppers
- 1 cup broccoli florets
- 1 cup snap peas
- 1/4 cup hoisin sauce
- 2 tbsp sesame seeds
- Cooked rice for serving

Directions:

1. In a bowl, combine cubed tofu, soy sauce, and cornstarch. Toss to coat the tofu evenly.

2. Preheat the air fryer to 200°C (390°F) and lightly grease the basket with vegetable oil.

3. Place the tofu in the air fryer basket and cook for 15 minutes, shaking the basket occasionally until the tofu is crispy.

4. While the tofu is cooking, heat 1 tablespoon of vegetable oil in a pan over medium heat.

5. Stir-fry the sliced bell peppers, broccoli, and snap peas for 5-7 minutes until they are tender.

6. Add the crispy tofu to the stir-fried vegetables and pour hoisin sauce over the mixture. Stir to coat everything evenly.

7. Serve the tofu and vegetable stir-fry over cooked rice and garnish with sesame seeds.

Nutrition Facts: (Per Serving)

- Calories: 320
- Fat: 18g
- Carbohydrates: 25g
- Protein: 18g

AIR-FRIED HONEY MUSTARD SALMON

Prep time: 10 mins | **Cook time:** 10 mins | **Total time:** 20 mins | **Servings:** 4

Ingredients:

- 4 salmon fillets
- 1/4 cup honey
- 2 tbsp Dijon mustard
- 1 tbsp whole-grain mustard
- 1 tbsp olive oil
- Salt and pepper to taste
- Lemon wedges for serving

Directions:

1. In a bowl, whisk together honey, Dijon mustard, whole-grain mustard, olive oil, salt, and pepper to make the honey mustard sauce.

2. Preheat the air fryer to 200°C (390°F) and lightly grease the basket.

3. Brush both sides of the salmon fillets with the honey mustard sauce.

4. Place the salmon fillets in the air fryer basket and cook for 10 minutes until the salmon is cooked through and flakes easily.

5. Serve the honey mustard salmon with lemon wedges for added freshness.

Nutrition Facts: (Per Serving)

- Calories: 320
- Fat: 14g
- Carbohydrates: 14g
- Protein: 35g

AIR-FRIED STUFFED BELL PEPPERS WITH GROUND BEEF

Prep time: 30 mins | **Cook time:** 30 mins | **Total time:** 1 hr | **Servings:** 4

Ingredients:

- 4 large bell peppers
- 1/2 pound ground beef
- 1 cup cooked rice
- 1/2 cup diced tomatoes
- 1/2 cup diced onions
- 1/2 cup shredded cheddar cheese
- 1 tsp chili powder
- Salt and pepper to taste
- Cooking spray

Directions:

1. Cut the tops off the bell peppers and remove the seeds and membranes.

2. In a pan, cook ground beef over medium heat until browned. Drain any excess fat.

3. In a bowl, combine cooked ground beef, cooked rice, diced tomatoes, diced onions, shredded cheddar cheese, chili powder, salt, and pepper.

4. Stuff each bell pepper with the ground beef and rice mixture.

5. Preheat the air fryer to 180°C (360°F) and lightly grease the basket with cooking spray.

6. Place the stuffed bell peppers in the basket, ensuring they are not overcrowded.

7. Cook for 30 minutes until the peppers are tender and the filling is heated through.

8. Serve as a satisfying dinner.

Nutrition Facts: (Per Serving)

- Calories: 380
- Fat: 18g
- Carbohydrates: 27g
- Protein: 28g

SEAFOOD

AIR-FRIED SHRIMP SCAMPI

Prep time: 15 mins | **Cook time:** 10 mins | **Total time:** 25 mins | **Servings:** 4

Ingredients:

- 1 pound large shrimp, peeled and deveined
- 4 cloves garlic, minced
- Zest and juice of 1 lemon
- 2 tbsp white wine (optional)
- 2 tbsp olive oil
- 2 tbsp chopped fresh parsley
- Salt and pepper to taste
- Cooked pasta for serving

Directions:

1. In a bowl, combine minced garlic, lemon zest, lemon juice, white wine (if using), olive oil, chopped fresh parsley, salt, and pepper to make the scampi sauce.

2. Preheat the air fryer to 200°C (390°F).

3. Lightly grease the air fryer basket and place the shrimp in a single layer.

4. Cook for 5 minutes, turning halfway through, until the shrimp are pink and cooked.

5. Remove the shrimp from the air fryer and set aside.

6. In a pan, heat the scampi sauce over medium heat.

7. Add the cooked pasta and cooked shrimp to the pan and toss to coat everything in the sauce.

8. Serve the shrimp scampi over pasta.

Nutrition Facts: (Per Serving)

- Calories: 320
- Fat: 10g
- Carbohydrates: 24g
- Protein: 30g

AIR-FRIED LEMON GARLIC BUTTER SALMON

Prep time: 10 mins | **Cook time:** 10 mins | **Total time:** 20 mins | **Servings:** 4

Ingredients:

- 4 salmon fillets
- 4 cloves garlic, minced
- Zest and juice of 1 lemon
- 2 tbsp melted butter
- 2 tbsp chopped fresh parsley
- Salt and pepper to taste
- Lemon wedges for serving

Directions:

1. In a bowl, combine minced garlic, lemon zest, lemon juice, melted butter, chopped fresh parsley, salt, and pepper to make the lemon garlic butter sauce.

2. Preheat the air fryer to 200°C (390°F) and lightly grease the basket.

3. Brush both sides of the salmon fillets with the lemon garlic butter sauce.

4. Place the salmon fillets in the air fryer basket and cook for 10 minutes until the salmon is cooked through and flakes easily.

5. Serve the lemon garlic butter salmon with lemon wedges for extra zing.

Nutrition Facts: (Per Serving)

- Calories: 340
- Fat: 20g
- Carbohydrates: 2g
- Protein: 35g

AIR-FRIED COCONUT-CRUSTED TILAPIA

Prep time: 15 mins | **Cook time:** 15 mins | **Total time:** 30 mins | **Servings:** 4

Ingredients:

- 4 tilapia fillets
- 1/2 cup shredded coconut
- 1/2 cup breadcrumbs
- 1/2 tsp paprika
- 1/4 tsp cayenne pepper
- Salt and pepper to taste
- 2 eggs, beaten
- Cooking spray
- Mango salsa for serving

Directions:

1. In a bowl, combine shredded coconut, breadcrumbs, paprika, cayenne pepper, salt, and pepper.

2. Dip each tilapia fillet into beaten eggs, then coat with the coconut breadcrumb mixture, pressing the coating onto the fillets.

3. Preheat the air fryer to 200°C (390°F) and lightly grease the basket with cooking spray.

4. Place the tilapia fillets in the basket, ensuring they are not overcrowded.

5. Cook for 15 minutes until the tilapia is crispy and flakes easily.

6. Serve hot with mango salsa for a tropical twist.

Nutrition Facts: (Per Serving)

- Calories: 280
- Fat: 14g
- Carbohydrates: 14g
- Protein: 25g

AIR-FRIED CAJUN SHRIMP AND SAUSAGE

Prep time: 15 mins | **Cook time:** 15 mins | **Total time:** 30 mins | **Servings:** 4

Ingredients:

- 1 pound large shrimp, peeled and deveined
- 4 links Cajun-style sausage, sliced
- 2 cups bell peppers and onions, sliced
- 2 tbsp Cajun seasoning
- 2 tbsp olive oil
- Salt and pepper to taste
- Cooked rice for serving

Directions:

1. In a bowl, toss together shrimp, Cajun seasoning, olive oil, salt, and pepper.
2. Preheat the air fryer to 200°C (390°F).
3. Lightly grease the air fryer basket and place the shrimp in a single layer.
4. Cook for 5 minutes, turning halfway through, until the shrimp are pink and cooked.
5. Remove the shrimp from the air fryer and set aside.
6. In the same pan, add sliced sausage and sliced bell peppers and onions.
7. Cook for 10 minutes, stirring occasionally, until the sausage is browned and the vegetables are tender.
8. Return the cooked shrimp to the pan and toss everything together.
9. Serve the Cajun shrimp and sausage over cooked rice.

Nutrition Facts: (Per Serving)

- Calories: 420
- Fat: 25g
- Carbohydrates: 20g
- Protein: 28g

AIR-FRIED GARLIC BUTTER SCALLOPS

Prep time: 10 mins | **Cook time:** 5 mins | **Total time:** 15 mins | **Servings:** 4

Ingredients:

- 1 pound sea scallops
- 4 cloves garlic, minced
- 2 tbsp melted butter
- 2 tbsp chopped fresh parsley
- Salt and pepper to taste
- Lemon wedges for serving

Directions:

1. In a bowl, combine minced garlic, melted butter, chopped fresh parsley, salt, and pepper to make the garlic butter sauce.

2. Preheat the air fryer to 200°C (390°F) and lightly grease the basket.

3. Place the sea scallops in the air fryer basket.

4. Brush the scallops with the garlic butter sauce.

5. Cook for 5 minutes until the scallops are opaque and cooked through.

6. Serve the garlic butter scallops with lemon wedges for a burst of flavor.

Nutrition Facts: (Per Serving)

- Calories: 180
- Fat: 8g
- Carbohydrates: 4g
- Protein: 23g

AIR-FRIED COCONUT SHRIMP WITH MANGO SALSA

Prep time: 15 mins | **Cook time:** 10 mins | **Total time:** 25 mins | **Servings:** 4

Ingredients:

- 1 pound large shrimp, peeled and deveined
- 1 cup shredded coconut
- 1/2 cup breadcrumbs
- 1/2 tsp paprika
- Salt and pepper to taste
- 2 eggs, beaten
- Cooking spray
- Mango salsa for serving

Directions:

1. In a bowl, combine shredded coconut, breadcrumbs, paprika, salt, and pepper.

2. Dip each shrimp into beaten eggs, then coat with the coconut breadcrumb mixture, pressing the coating onto the shrimp.

3. Preheat the air fryer to 200°C (390°F) and lightly grease the basket with cooking spray.

4. Place the coconut shrimp in the basket, ensuring they are not overcrowded.

5. Cook for 10 minutes until the shrimp are crispy and golden.

6. Serve hot with mango salsa for a tropical twist.

Nutrition Facts: (Per Serving)

- Calories: 340
- Fat: 18g
- Carbohydrates: 18g
- Protein: 26g

AIR-FRIED LEMON BUTTER LOBSTER TAILS

Prep time: 15 mins | **Cook time:** 10 mins | **Total time:** 25 mins | **Servings:** 4

Ingredients:

- 4 lobster tails
- 1/2 cup melted butter
- Zest and juice of 1 lemon
- 2 cloves garlic, minced
- 2 tbsp chopped fresh parsley
- Salt and pepper to taste
- Lemon wedges for serving

Directions:

1. Using kitchen shears, cut the top of each lobster tail lengthwise and pull the meat up through the opening.

2. In a bowl, combine melted butter, lemon zest, lemon juice, minced garlic, chopped fresh parsley, salt, and pepper to make the lemon butter sauce.

3. Preheat the air fryer to 200°C (390°F).

4. Place the lobster tails in the air fryer basket.

5. Brush the lobster meat with the lemon butter sauce.

6. Cook for 10 minutes until the lobster meat is opaque and cooked through.

7. Serve the lemon butter lobster tails with lemon wedges for added flavor.

Nutrition Facts: (Per Serving)

- Calories: 280
- Fat: 18g
- Carbohydrates: 2g
- Protein: 26g

AIR-FRIED TERIYAKI SALMON SKEWERS

Prep time: 20 mins | **Cook time:** 10 mins | **Total time:** 30 mins | **Servings:** 4

Ingredients:

- 4 salmon fillets, cut into cubes
- 1/4 cup teriyaki sauce
- 2 tbsp honey
- 1 tbsp sesame oil
- 1 tsp grated ginger
- 2 cloves garlic, minced
- Wooden skewers, soaked in water
- Sesame seeds and chopped green onions for garnish

Directions:

1. In a bowl, whisk together teriyaki sauce, honey, sesame oil, grated ginger, and minced garlic to make the teriyaki marinade.

2. Thread salmon cubes onto soaked wooden skewers.

3. Place the salmon skewers in a shallow dish and pour the teriyaki marinade over them. Let them marinate for 10 minutes.

4. Preheat the air fryer to 200°C (390°F).

5. Lightly grease the air fryer basket and place the salmon skewers in a single layer.

6. Air-fry for 10 minutes, turning halfway through, until the salmon is cooked and slightly caramelized.

7. Garnish with sesame seeds and chopped green onions before serving.

Nutrition Facts: (Per Serving)

- Calories: 320
- Fat: 14g
- Carbohydrates: 14g
- Protein: 30g

AIR-FRIED CAJUN CATFISH

Prep time: 15 mins | **Cook time:** 10 mins | **Total time:** 25 mins | **Servings:** 4

Ingredients:

- 4 catfish fillets
- 2 tbsp Cajun seasoning
- 2 tbsp olive oil
- Salt and pepper to taste
- Lemon wedges for serving

Directions:

1. In a bowl, toss catfish fillets with Cajun seasoning, olive oil, salt, and pepper to coat them evenly.

2. Preheat the air fryer to 200°C (390°F).

3. Lightly grease the air fryer basket and place the catfish fillets in a single layer.

4. Cook for 10 minutes until the catfish is crispy and cooked through.

5. Serve with lemon wedges for a zesty kick.

Nutrition Facts: (Per Serving)

- Calories: 290
- Fat: 15g
- Carbohydrates: 2g
- Protein: 36g

AIR-FRIED SCALLOP AND ASPARAGUS STIR-FRY

Prep time: 15 mins | **Cook time:** 10 mins | **Total time:** 25 mins | **Servings:** 4

Ingredients:

- 1 pound sea scallops
- 1 bunch asparagus, trimmed and cut into pieces
- 1 red bell pepper, sliced
- 1/4 cup low-sodium soy sauce
- 2 tbsp honey
- 1 tbsp sesame oil
- 2 cloves garlic, minced
- 1 tsp grated ginger
- Sesame seeds for garnish

Directions:

1. In a bowl, whisk together low-sodium soy sauce, honey, sesame oil, minced garlic, and grated ginger to make the stir-fry sauce.

2. Preheat the air fryer to 200°C (390°F).

3. Lightly grease the air fryer basket and place scallops, asparagus, and red bell pepper inside.

4. Pour the stir-fry sauce over the ingredients in the basket.

5. Cook for 10 minutes, stirring halfway through, until the scallops are opaque and the vegetables are tender-crisp.

6. Garnish with sesame seeds before serving.

Nutrition Facts: (Per Serving)

- Calories: 220
- Fat: 6g
- Carbohydrates: 18g
- Protein: 24g

SIDE DISHES

AIR-FRIED GARLIC
PARMESAN ASPARAGUS

Prep time: 10 mins | **Cook time:** 10 mins | **Total time:** 20 mins | **Servings:** 4

Ingredients:

- 1 bunch asparagus, trimmed
- 2 tbsp olive oil
- 2 cloves garlic, minced
- 1/4 cup grated Parmesan cheese
- Salt and pepper to taste
- Lemon wedges for serving

Directions:

1. In a bowl, toss asparagus with olive oil, minced garlic, grated Parmesan cheese, salt, and pepper.

2. Preheat the air fryer to 200°C (390°F).

3. Place the seasoned asparagus in the air fryer basket.

4. Cook for 10 minutes until the asparagus is tender-crisp and lightly browned.

5. Serve the garlic Parmesan asparagus with lemon wedges for added zing.

Nutrition Facts: (Per Serving)

- Calories: 90
- Fat: 7g
- Carbohydrates: 4g
- Protein: 4g

AIR-FRIED SWEET POTATO FRIES

Prep time: 15 mins | **Cook time:** 20 mins | **Total time:** 35 mins | **Servings:** 4

Ingredients:

- 2 large sweet potatoes, cut into fries
- 2 tbsp olive oil
- 1 tsp paprika
- 1/2 tsp garlic powder
- 1/2 tsp onion powder
- Salt and pepper to taste
- Cooking spray

Directions:

1. In a bowl, toss sweet potato fries with olive oil, paprika, garlic powder, onion powder, salt, and pepper.

2. Preheat the air fryer to 200°C (390°F).

3. Lightly grease the air fryer basket with cooking spray and place the sweet potato fries in a single layer.

4. Cook for 20 minutes, shaking the basket occasionally, until the fries are crispy and golden.

5. Serve the sweet potato fries as a delicious side dish.

Nutrition Facts: (Per Serving)

- Calories: 180
- Fat: 7g
- Carbohydrates: 28g
- Protein: 2g

AIR-FRIED BRUSSELS SPROUTS

Prep time: 10 mins | **Cook time:** 15 mins | **Total time:** 25 mins | **Servings:** 4

Ingredients:

- 1 pound Brussels sprouts, trimmed and halved
- 2 tbsp olive oil
- 2 cloves garlic, minced
- 1/4 cup grated Parmesan cheese
- Salt and pepper to taste
- Lemon wedges for serving

Directions:

1. In a bowl, toss Brussels sprouts with olive oil, minced garlic, grated Parmesan cheese, salt, and pepper.

2. Preheat the air fryer to 200°C (390°F).

3. Place the seasoned Brussels sprouts in the air fryer basket.

4. Cook for 15 minutes until the Brussels sprouts are tender and crispy.

5. Serve the garlic Parmesan Brussels sprouts with lemon wedges for extra flavor.

Nutrition Facts: (Per Serving)

- Calories: 100
- Fat: 7g
- Carbohydrates: 7g
- Protein: 4g

AIR-FRIED ZUCCHINI CHIPS

Prep time: 15 mins | **Cook time:** 15 mins | **Total time:** 30 mins | **Servings:** 4

Ingredients:

- 2 large zucchinis, sliced into chips
- 1/2 cup breadcrumbs
- 1/4 cup grated Parmesan cheese
- 1/2 tsp garlic powder
- 1/2 tsp onion powder
- Salt and pepper to taste
- 2 eggs, beaten
- Cooking spray

Directions:

1. In a bowl, combine breadcrumbs, grated Parmesan cheese, garlic powder, onion powder, salt, and pepper.

2. Dip each zucchini chip into beaten eggs, then coat with the breadcrumb mixture, pressing the coating onto the chips.

3. Preheat the air fryer to 200°C (390°F) and lightly grease the basket with cooking spray.

4. Place the zucchini chips in the basket, ensuring they are not overcrowded.

5. Cook for 15 minutes until the zucchini chips are crispy and golden.

6. Serve as a healthy and tasty side dish.

Nutrition Facts: (Per Serving)

- Calories: 160
- Fat: 7g
- Carbohydrates: 20g
- Protein: 7g

AIR-FRIED CORN ON THE COB

Prep time: 10 mins | **Cook time:** 15 mins | **Total time:** 25 mins | **Servings:** 4

Ingredients:

- 4 ears of corn, husked
- 2 tbsp melted butter
- 1/2 tsp smoked paprika
- Salt and pepper to taste

Directions:

1. In a bowl, combine melted butter, smoked paprika, salt, and pepper.
2. Preheat the air fryer to 200°C (390°F).
3. Place the ears of corn in the air fryer basket.
4. Brush the corn with the seasoned butter mixture.
5. Cook for 15 minutes, turning halfway through, until the corn is tender and slightly charred.
6. Serve the air-fried corn on the cob as a delightful side dish.

Nutrition Facts: (Per Serving)

- Calories: 140
- Fat: 7g
- Carbohydrates: 19g
- Protein: 3g

AIR-FRIED GARLIC PARMESAN GREEN BEANS

Prep time: 10 mins | **Cook time:** 10 mins | **Total time:** 20 mins | **Servings:** 4

Ingredients:

- 1 pound fresh green beans, trimmed
- 2 tbsp olive oil
- 2 cloves garlic, minced
- 1/4 cup grated Parmesan cheese
- Salt and pepper to taste
- Lemon wedges for serving

Directions:

1. In a bowl, toss green beans with olive oil, minced garlic, grated Parmesan cheese, salt, and pepper.
2. Preheat the air fryer to 200°C (390°F).
3. Place the seasoned green beans in the air fryer basket.
4. Cook for 10 minutes until the green beans are tender-crisp and slightly charred.
5. Serve with lemon wedges for an extra burst of flavor.

Nutrition Facts: (Per Serving)

- Calories: 110
- Fat: 7g
- Carbohydrates: 8g
- Protein: 4g

AIR-FRIED HERB-ROASTED POTATOES

Prep time: 15 mins | **Cook time:** 20 mins | **Total time:** 35 mins | **Servings:** 4

Ingredients:

- 1 pound baby potatoes, halved
- 2 tbsp olive oil
- 1 tsp dried rosemary
- 1 tsp dried thyme
- Salt and pepper to taste
- Chopped fresh parsley for garnish

Directions:

1. In a bowl, toss baby potatoes with olive oil, dried rosemary, dried thyme, salt, and pepper.

2. Preheat the air fryer to 200°C (390°F).

3. Place the seasoned potatoes in the air fryer basket.

4. Cook for 20 minutes, shaking the basket occasionally, until the potatoes are crispy and golden.

5. Garnish with chopped fresh parsley before serving.

Nutrition Facts: (Per Serving)

- Calories: 160
- Fat: 7g
- Carbohydrates: 23g
- Protein: 2g

AIR-FRIED BALSAMIC BRUSSELS SPROUTS

Prep time: 10 mins | **Cook time:** 15 mins | **Total time:** 25 mins | **Servings:** 4

Ingredients:

- 1 pound Brussels sprouts, trimmed and halved
- 2 tbsp olive oil
- 2 tbsp balsamic vinegar
- 1 clove garlic, minced
- Salt and pepper to taste
- Grated Parmesan cheese for garnish

Directions:

1. In a bowl, toss Brussels sprouts with olive oil, balsamic vinegar, minced garlic, salt, and pepper.

2. Preheat the air fryer to 200°C (390°F).

3. Place the seasoned Brussels sprouts in the air fryer basket.

4. Cook for 15 minutes until the Brussels sprouts are tender-crisp and caramelized.

5. Sprinkle with grated Parmesan cheese before serving.

Nutrition Facts: (Per Serving)

- Calories: 90
- Fat: 5g
- Carbohydrates: 11g
- Protein: 3g

AIR-FRIED GARLIC MASHED POTATOES

Prep time: 15 mins | **Cook time:** 15 mins | **Total time:** 30 mins | **Servings:** 4

Ingredients:

- 4 large potatoes, peeled and diced
- 2 cloves garlic, minced
- 2 tbsp butter
- 1/4 cup milk
- Salt and pepper to taste
- Chopped fresh chives for garnish

Directions:

1. Place diced potatoes in a microwave-safe bowl, cover with water, and microwave for 8-10 minutes until tender.

2. Drain the potatoes and transfer them to a bowl.

3. In a small saucepan, melt butter and sauté minced garlic until fragrant.

4. Mash the cooked potatoes, adding the garlic butter, milk, salt, and pepper.

5. Preheat the air fryer to 180°C (360°F).

6. Place the mashed potatoes in an oven-safe dish and smooth the top.

7. Air-fry for 15 minutes until the top is golden brown.

8. Garnish with chopped fresh chives before serving.

Nutrition Facts: (Per Serving)

- Calories: 180
- Fat: 5g
- Carbohydrates: 31g
- Protein: 4g

AIR-FRIED RATATOUILLE

Prep time: 20 mins | **Cook time:** 20 mins | **Total time:** 40 mins | **Servings:** 4

Ingredients:

- 1 small eggplant, diced
- 2 small zucchinis, diced
- 2 red bell peppers, diced
- 2 tomatoes, diced
- 1 onion, diced
- 2 cloves garlic, minced
- 2 tbsp olive oil
- 1 tsp dried basil
- 1 tsp dried thyme
- Salt and pepper to taste
- Grated Parmesan cheese for garnish

Directions:

1. In a large bowl, toss diced eggplant, zucchinis, red bell peppers, tomatoes, onion, and minced garlic with olive oil, dried basil, dried thyme, salt, and pepper.

2. Preheat the air fryer to 180°C (360°F).

3. Place the seasoned vegetables in the air fryer basket.

4. Cook for 20 minutes, shaking the basket occasionally, until the vegetables are tender and slightly caramelized.

5. Garnish with grated Parmesan cheese before serving.

Nutrition Facts: (Per Serving)

- Calories: 110
- Fat: 7g
- Carbohydrates: 12g
- Protein: 2g

POULTRY

AIR-FRIED BUTTERMILK FRIED CHICKEN

Prep time: 30 mins | **Cook time:** 20 mins | **Total time:** 50 mins | **Servings:** 4

Ingredients:

- 4 bone-in chicken thighs
- 1 cup buttermilk
- 1 cup all-purpose flour
- 1 tsp paprika
- 1 tsp garlic powder
- Salt and pepper to taste
- Cooking spray

Directions:

1. In a bowl, combine buttermilk, paprika, garlic powder, salt, and pepper.

2. Place chicken thighs in the buttermilk mixture and let them marinate for 30 minutes.

3. Preheat the air fryer to 180°C (360°F).

4. In a separate bowl, mix flour, salt, and pepper.

5. Remove the chicken from the buttermilk, allowing excess to drip off, and coat each piece with the flour mixture.

6. Lightly spray the chicken with cooking spray and place them in the air fryer basket.

7. Cook for 20 minutes, turning halfway through, until the chicken is crispy and cooked through.

Nutrition Facts: (Per Serving)

- Calories: 350
- Fat: 15g
- Carbohydrates: 30g
- Protein: 24g

AIR-FRIED LEMON PEPPER CHICKEN WINGS

Prep time: 15 mins | **Cook time:** 20 mins | **Total time:** 35 mins | **Servings:** 4

Ingredients:

- 1 pound chicken wings
- 2 tbsp olive oil
- 1 tbsp lemon pepper seasoning
- 1 tsp garlic powder
- Salt to taste
- Lemon wedges for serving

Directions:

1. In a bowl, toss chicken wings with olive oil, lemon pepper seasoning, garlic powder, and salt.

2. Preheat the air fryer to 200°C (390°F).

3. Place the seasoned chicken wings in the air fryer basket.

4. Cook for 20 minutes until the wings are golden brown and crispy.

5. Serve with lemon wedges for a zesty touch.

Nutrition Facts: (Per Serving)

- Calories: 280
- Fat: 20g
- Carbohydrates: 1g
- Protein: 22g

AIR-FRIED HONEY MUSTARD CHICKEN TENDERS

Prep time: 15 mins | **Cook time:** 15 mins | **Total time:** 30 mins | **Servings:** 4

Ingredients:

- 1 pound chicken tenders
- 1/4 cup honey
- 2 tbsp Dijon mustard
- 1 tbsp olive oil
- 1 tsp garlic powder
- Salt and pepper to taste

Directions:

1. In a bowl, whisk together honey, Dijon mustard, olive oil, garlic powder, salt, and pepper.

2. Place chicken tenders in the honey mustard mixture and let them marinate for 15 minutes.

3. Preheat the air fryer to 180°C (360°F).

4. Place the marinated chicken tenders in the air fryer basket.

5. Cook for 15 minutes until the chicken is cooked through and has a crispy exterior.

Nutrition Facts: (Per Serving)

- Calories: 280
- Fat: 10g
- Carbohydrates: 19g
- Protein: 26g

AIR-FRIED BUFFALO CHICKEN TACOS

Prep time: 20 mins | **Cook time:** 15 mins | **Total time:** 35 mins | **Servings:** 4

Ingredients:

- 1 pound boneless, skinless chicken breasts
- 1/4 cup hot sauce
- 2 tbsp melted butter
- 1 tsp garlic powder
- 1/2 tsp onion powder
- 1/2 tsp paprika
- 1/2 tsp cayenne pepper (adjust to taste)
- 8 small flour tortillas
- 1 cup shredded lettuce
- 1/2 cup diced tomatoes
- 1/4 cup diced red onion
- Ranch or blue cheese dressing for drizzling

Directions:

1. In a bowl, combine hot sauce, melted butter, garlic powder, onion powder, paprika, and cayenne pepper to make the buffalo sauce.

2. Slice chicken breasts into thin strips and toss them in the buffalo sauce until well coated.

3. Preheat the air fryer to 200°C (390°F).

4. Place the buffalo chicken strips in the air fryer basket and cook for 15 minutes, turning halfway through, until crispy.

5. Warm the tortillas.

6. Assemble tacos with shredded lettuce, diced tomatoes, buffalo chicken strips, diced red onion, and a drizzle of ranch or blue cheese dressing.

Nutrition Facts: (Per Serving)

- Calories: 390
- Fat: 14g
- Carbohydrates: 34g
- Protein: 30g

AIR-FRIED HERB-CRUSTED TURKEY BREAST

Prep time: 15 mins | **Cook time:** 45 mins | **Total time:** 1 hour | **Servings:** 4

Ingredients:

- 1 boneless turkey breast
- 2 tbsp olive oil
- 1 tbsp dried thyme
- 1 tbsp dried rosemary
- 1 tbsp dried sage
- 1 tsp garlic powder
- Salt and pepper to taste

Directions:

1. In a bowl, mix olive oil, dried thyme, dried rosemary, dried sage, garlic powder, salt, and pepper to create a herb crust.

2. Rub the herb crust all over the turkey breast.

3. Preheat the air fryer to 180°C (360°F).

4. Place the turkey breast in the air fryer basket.

5. Cook for 45 minutes until the turkey is cooked through and the herb crust is crispy.

Nutrition Facts: (Per Serving)

- Calories: 250
- Fat: 10g
- Carbohydrates: 1g
- Protein: 35g

AIR-FRIED CRANBERRY PECAN STUFFED CHICKEN BREAST

Prep time: 20 mins | **Cook time:** 25 mins | **Total time:** 45 mins | **Servings:** 4

Ingredients:

- 4 boneless, skinless chicken breasts
- 1/2 cup dried cranberries
- 1/4 cup chopped pecans
- 2 tbsp cream cheese
- 1 tsp dried thyme
- 1/2 tsp garlic powder
- Salt and pepper to taste
- Cooking twine

Directions:

1. In a bowl, combine dried cranberries, chopped pecans, cream cheese, dried thyme, garlic powder, salt, and pepper.

2. Carefully butterfly each chicken breast by slicing horizontally, creating a pocket.

3. Stuff each chicken breast with the cranberry pecan mixture and secure with cooking twine.

4. Preheat the air fryer to 180°C (360°F).

5. Place the stuffed chicken breasts in the air fryer basket.

6. Cook for 25 minutes until the chicken is cooked through and the outside is golden and crispy.

Nutrition Facts: (Per Serving)

- Calories: 320
- Fat: 12g
- Carbohydrates: 16g
- Protein: 35g

AIR-FRIED TANDOORI CHICKEN SKEWERS

Prep time: 20 mins | **Cook time:** 15 mins | **Total time:** 35 mins | **Servings:** 4

Ingredients:

- 1 pound chicken breast, cut into cubes
- 1/2 cup plain yogurt
- 2 tbsp tandoori seasoning
- 2 cloves garlic, minced
- 1 tsp grated ginger
- Juice of 1 lemon
- Salt and pepper to taste
- Wooden skewers, soaked in water

Directions:

1. In a bowl, mix plain yogurt, tandoori seasoning, minced garlic, grated ginger, lemon juice, salt, and pepper to make the marinade.

2. Thread chicken cubes onto soaked wooden skewers.

3. Coat the chicken skewers with the tandoori marinade.

4. Preheat the air fryer to 200°C (390°F).

5. Place the chicken skewers in the air fryer basket.

6. Cook for 15 minutes until the chicken is cooked through and has a slight char.

Nutrition Facts: (Per Serving)

- Calories: 220
- Fat: 5g
- Carbohydrates: 7g
- Protein: 35g

AIR-FRIED PESTO STUFFED CHICKEN THIGHS

Prep time: 20 mins | **Cook time:** 25 mins | **Total time:** 45 mins | **Servings:** 4

Ingredients:

- 4 boneless, skinless chicken thighs
- 1/4 cup pesto sauce
- 1/2 cup mozzarella cheese, shredded
- Salt and pepper to taste
- Cooking spray

Directions:

1. Using a sharp knife, make a pocket in each chicken thigh.
2. Stuff each pocket with pesto sauce and mozzarella cheese, then secure with toothpicks.
3. Preheat the air fryer to 180°C (360°F).
4. Lightly grease the air fryer basket with cooking spray.
5. Place the stuffed chicken thighs in the basket.
6. Cook for 25 minutes until the chicken is cooked through, and the cheese is melted and bubbly.

Nutrition Facts: (Per Serving)

- Calories: 320
- Fat: 22g
- Carbohydrates: 2g
- Protein: 27g

AIR-FRIED ORANGE GLAZED DUCK BREAST

Prep time: 15 mins | **Cook time:** 25 mins | **Total time:** 40 mins | **Servings:** 4

Ingredients:

- 4 duck breasts
- Zest and juice of 2 oranges
- 1/4 cup honey
- 2 tbsp soy sauce
- 1 tsp ginger, minced
- Salt and pepper to taste

Directions:

1. In a bowl, whisk together orange zest, orange juice, honey, soy sauce, minced ginger, salt, and pepper to make the orange glaze.

2. Score the duck breast skin in a crosshatch pattern, being careful not to cut into the meat.

3. Preheat the air fryer to 180°C (360°F).

4. Place the duck breasts skin-side down in the air fryer basket.

5. Cook for 15 minutes, then flip the duck breasts.

6. Brush the orange glaze over the duck breasts and cook for an additional 10 minutes or until the duck is cooked to your desired level of doneness.

Nutrition Facts: (Per Serving)

- Calories: 320
- Fat: 22g
- Carbohydrates: 14g
- Protein: 20g

AIR-FRIED BBQ CHICKEN DRUMSTICKS

Prep time: 15 mins | **Cook time:** 30 mins | **Total time:** 45 mins | **Servings:** 4

Ingredients:

- 8 chicken drumsticks
- 1/2 cup BBQ sauce
- 2 tbsp olive oil
- 1 tsp smoked paprika
- 1/2 tsp onion powder
- Salt and pepper to taste

Directions:

1. In a bowl, mix BBQ sauce, olive oil, smoked paprika, onion powder, salt, and pepper to create a marinade.

2. Coat the chicken drumsticks with the marinade and let them sit for 15 minutes.

3. Preheat the air fryer to 200°C (390°F).

4. Place the marinated chicken drumsticks in the air fryer basket.

5. Cook for 30 minutes, turning them halfway through, until the chicken is cooked through and the skin is crispy.

Nutrition Facts: (Per Serving)

- Calories: 320
- Fat: 15g
- Carbohydrates: 18g
- Protein: 25g

DESSERTS

AIR-FRIED APPLE HAND PIES

Prep time: 20 mins | **Cook time:** 10 mins | **Total time:** 30 mins | **Servings:** 4

Ingredients:

- 2 sheets of puff pastry, thawed
- 2 cups diced apples
- 1/4 cup granulated sugar
- 1/2 tsp ground cinnamon
- 1/4 tsp ground nutmeg
- 1 egg, beaten
- Icing sugar for dusting

Directions:

1. In a bowl, combine diced apples, granulated sugar, ground cinnamon, and ground nutmeg to make the apple filling.

2. Roll out the puff pastry sheets and cut them into squares.

3. Place a spoonful of apple filling in the center of each pastry square.

4. Fold the squares in half to form triangles and press the edges to seal.

5. Brush the tops of the hand pies with beaten egg.

6. Preheat the air fryer to 180°C (360°F).

7. Place the hand pies in the air fryer basket, ensuring they are not touching.

8. Cook for 10 minutes until the hand pies are golden brown and flaky.

9. Dust with icing sugar before serving.

Nutrition Facts: (Per Serving)

- Calories: 320
- Fat: 15g
- Carbohydrates: 42g
- Protein: 4g

AIR-FRIED BANANA FRITTERS

Prep time: 15 mins | **Cook time:** 10 mins | **Total time:** 25 mins | **Servings:** 4

Ingredients:

- 4 ripe bananas, sliced
- 1/2 cup plain flour
- 1/4 cup cornflour
- 2 tbsp granulated sugar
- 1/2 tsp baking powder
- 1/4 tsp salt
- 1/2 cup water
- Cooking oil for spraying

Directions:

1. In a bowl, combine plain flour, cornflour, granulated sugar, baking powder, and salt.

2. Add water to the dry ingredients and whisk until you have a smooth batter.

3. Dip banana slices into the batter, ensuring they are well coated.

4. Preheat the air fryer to 180°C (360°F) and lightly grease the basket with cooking oil.

5. Place the banana fritters in the air fryer basket, ensuring they are not touching.

6. Spray the tops of the fritters with a little more cooking oil.

7. Cook for 10 minutes until the banana fritters are crispy and golden.

8. Serve as a delightful dessert.

Nutrition Facts: (Per Serving)

- Calories: 230
- Fat: 1g
- Carbohydrates: 57g
- Protein: 2g

AIR-FRIED CHOCOLATE CHIP COOKIES

Prep time: 15 mins | **Cook time:** 10 mins | **Total time:** 25 mins | **Servings:** 4

Ingredients:

- 1/2 cup unsalted butter, softened
- 1/2 cup granulated sugar
- 1/4 cup brown sugar
- 1 egg
- 1 tsp vanilla extract
- 1 1/4 cups plain flour
- 1/2 tsp baking soda
- 1/4 tsp salt
- 1/2 cup chocolate chips

Directions:

1. In a bowl, cream together softened butter, granulated sugar, and brown sugar until light and fluffy.

2. Beat in the egg and vanilla extract.

3. In a separate bowl, whisk together plain flour, baking soda, and salt.

4. Gradually add the dry ingredients to the wet ingredients and mix until a cookie dough forms.

5. Fold in the chocolate chips.

6. Preheat the air fryer to 180°C (360°F).

7. Drop spoonfuls of cookie dough onto a greased tray that fits into the air fryer.

8. Place the tray in the air fryer basket.

9. Cook for 10 minutes until the chocolate chip cookies are golden brown.

10. Allow them to cool slightly before enjoying.

Nutrition Facts: (Per Serving)

- Calories: 380
- Fat: 19g
- Carbohydrates: 51g
- Protein: 4g

AIR-FRIED CINNAMON SUGAR DONUTS

Prep time: 15 mins | **Cook time:** 10 mins | **Total time:** 25 mins | **Servings:** 4

Ingredients:

- 1 tube refrigerated biscuit dough
- 1/4 cup granulated sugar
- 1 tsp ground cinnamon
- Cooking spray
- Icing sugar for dusting

Directions:

1. Separate the biscuit dough into individual biscuits.

2. In a bowl, combine granulated sugar and ground cinnamon.

3. Roll each biscuit into a ball and dip it into the cinnamon sugar mixture to coat it.

4. Preheat the air fryer to 180°C (360°F) and lightly grease the basket with cooking spray.

5. Place the coated biscuit balls in the air fryer basket, ensuring they are not touching.

6. Cook for 10 minutes until the donuts are golden brown and cooked through.

7. Dust with icing sugar before serving.

Nutrition Facts: (Per Serving)

- Calories: 240
- Fat: 7g
- Carbohydrates: 42g
- Protein: 2g

AIR-FRIED STRAWBERRY SHORTCAKE

Prep time: 15 mins | **Cook time:** 10 mins | **Total time:** 25 mins | **Servings:** 4

Ingredients:

- 1 sheet of puff pastry, thawed
- 1 cup fresh strawberries, sliced
- 1/4 cup granulated sugar
- 1/2 cup whipped cream
- Icing sugar for dusting

Directions:

1. Preheat the air fryer to 180°C (360°F).

2. Cut the puff pastry into squares and place them in the air fryer basket, ensuring they are not touching.

3. Cook for 10 minutes until the puff pastry squares are golden brown and puffed up.

4. In a bowl, toss fresh strawberries with granulated sugar and let them macerate.

5. Allow the puff pastry squares to cool slightly, then slice them in half horizontally.

6. Spoon macerated strawberries onto the bottom half of each puff pastry square.

7. Top with whipped cream and place the other half of the puff pastry on top.

8. Dust with icing sugar before serving.

Nutrition Facts: (Per Serving)

- Calories: 280
- Fat: 15g
- Carbohydrates: 32g
- Protein: 3g

AIR-FRIED BANANA CHOCOLATE SPRING ROLLS

Prep time: 15 mins | **Cook time:** 10 mins | **Total time:** 25 mins | **Servings:** 4

Ingredients:

- 4 sheets of spring roll wrappers
- 2 ripe bananas, sliced
- 1/2 cup chocolate chips
- Cooking spray
- Icing sugar for dusting

Directions:

1. Place a few banana slices and a sprinkle of chocolate chips on each spring roll wrapper.

2. Roll up the wrappers, tucking in the sides as you go, to form spring rolls.

3. Preheat the air fryer to 180°C (360°F).

4. Lightly grease the air fryer basket with cooking spray and place the spring rolls in a single layer.

5. Cook for 10 minutes until the spring rolls are golden brown and crispy.

6. Dust with icing sugar before serving.

Nutrition Facts: (Per Serving)

- Calories: 250
- Fat: 8g
- Carbohydrates: 42g
- Protein: 4g

AIR-FRIED CARAMELIZED PINEAPPLE

Prep time: 10 mins | **Cook time:** 10 mins | **Total time:** 20 mins | **Servings:** 4

Ingredients:

- 1 pineapple, peeled, cored, and sliced into rings
- 1/4 cup brown sugar
- 1 tsp ground cinnamon
- Cooking spray
- Vanilla ice cream for serving

Directions:

1. In a bowl, combine brown sugar and ground cinnamon.

2. Lightly spray the pineapple rings with cooking spray.

3. Coat each pineapple ring with the brown sugar and cinnamon mixture.

4. Preheat the air fryer to 200°C (390°F).

5. Place the pineapple rings in the air fryer basket.

6. Cook for 10 minutes until the pineapple is caramelized and slightly charred.

7. Serve the caramelized pineapple with a scoop of vanilla ice cream for a delightful dessert.

Nutrition Facts: (Per Serving)

- Calories: 160
- Fat: 0g
- Carbohydrates: 41g
- Protein: 1g

AIR-FRIED RASPBERRY CHOCOLATE TARTS

Prep time: 20 mins | **Cook time:** 15 mins | **Total time:** 35 mins | **Servings:** 4

Ingredients:

- 4 sheets of puff pastry, thawed
- 1/2 cup fresh raspberries
- 1/4 cup chocolate chips
- 2 tbsp honey
- Cooking spray
- Icing sugar for dusting

Directions:

1. Preheat the air fryer to 180°C (360°F).

2. Cut the puff pastry into squares and place them in the air fryer basket, ensuring they are not touching.

3. Cook for 15 minutes until the puff pastry squares are golden brown and puffed up.

4. Remove the puff pastry squares from the air fryer.

5. Top each square with fresh raspberries and a sprinkle of chocolate chips.

6. Drizzle honey over the tarts.

7. Dust with icing sugar before serving.

Nutrition Facts: (Per Serving)

- Calories: 280
- Fat: 14g
- Carbohydrates: 38g
- Protein: 3g

AIR-FRIED BLUEBERRY LEMON CHEESECAKE

Prep time: 15 mins | **Cook time:** 25 mins | **Total time:** 40 mins | **Servings:** 4

Ingredients:

- 8 oz cream cheese, softened
- 1/2 cup granulated sugar
- 1 egg
- 1 tsp vanilla extract
- Zest and juice of 1 lemon
- 1/2 cup fresh blueberries
- Graham cracker crumbs for garnish

Directions:

1. In a bowl, beat softened cream cheese and granulated sugar until smooth.
2. Add the egg, vanilla extract, lemon zest, and lemon juice, and mix until well combined.
3. Preheat the air fryer to 160°C (320°F).
4. Line a small baking dish that fits in the air fryer with parchment paper.
5. Pour the cream cheese mixture into the dish.
6. Sprinkle fresh blueberries evenly over the top.
7. Air-fry for 25 minutes until the cheesecake is set and slightly golden.
8. Remove from the air fryer and let it cool.
9. Garnish with graham cracker crumbs before serving.

Nutrition Facts: (Per Serving)

- Calories: 350
- Fat: 24g
- Carbohydrates: 28g
- Protein: 5g

AIR-FRIED PEAR AND ALMOND PHYLLO CUPS

Prep time: 20 mins | **Cook time:** 10 mins | **Total time:** 30 mins | **Servings:** 4

Ingredients:

- 4 sheets of phyllo pastry
- 2 ripe pears, thinly sliced
- 1/4 cup almond paste
- 2 tbsp honey
- Cooking spray
- Chopped almonds for garnish

Directions:

1. Preheat the air fryer to 180°C (360°F).

2. Lightly grease four small ramekins with cooking spray.

3. Layer one sheet of phyllo pastry in each ramekin, allowing it to overhang the edges.

4. Spread almond paste evenly over the phyllo pastry.

5. Place thinly sliced pears on top of the almond paste.

6. Drizzle honey over the pears.

7. Fold the overhanging phyllo pastry over the pears.

8. Lightly spray the tops with cooking spray.

9. Air-fry for 10 minutes until the phyllo cups are golden brown and crisp.

10. Garnish with chopped almonds before serving.

Nutrition Facts: (Per Serving)

- Calories: 320
- Fat: 14g
- Carbohydrates: 48g
- Protein: 5g

CONCLUSION

As we wrap up this culinary adventure through the world of air frying, we want to extend our heartfelt gratitude to you, our readers, for embarking on this journey with us. We hope this Air Fryer Cookbook has ignited your passion for healthier, more delicious cooking and empowered you to make the most of your air fryer.

Throughout this book, we've explored the ins and outs of air frying, from understanding the mechanics of this remarkable appliance to uncovering the countless benefits it brings to your kitchen. We've shared essential cooking tips, maintenance advice, and a diverse array of delectable recipes that cater to a wide range of tastes and preferences.

As you continue your culinary adventures with your air fryer, remember that experimentation is key. Don't hesitate to get creative in the kitchen, trying out new ingredients and flavor combinations. With the knowledge and skills you've acquired from this cookbook, you're well-equipped to craft meals that will tantalize your taste buds and leave your loved ones asking for more.

In the world of cooking, there's always something new to learn and discover. We encourage you to keep exploring, honing your skills, and sharing your culinary creations with friends and family. The air fryer is your trusty companion on this culinary journey, ready to help you achieve crispy perfection with every dish you prepare.

Once again, thank you for choosing this Air Fryer Cookbook as your guide. We wish you many happy hours of cooking and sharing delicious meals with your loved ones. May your kitchen always be filled with the delightful aroma of crispy, golden goodness. Happy air frying!

Printed in Great Britain
by Amazon